Praise for *Hunt with You~~r Pack~~*

"I am privileged to watch Kay work her mastery across the years and with scores of clients. With as much as she accomplished, one might not suspect that she needed to unlock an unconventional approach to business development and client service. Her approach is not some new and improved method. Rather, with vulnerability, she walks us through her process of figuring it out as someone more introverted and more able to see patterns in data than in people. There is hope for all of us who don't fit a hard-charging, effusive approach to developing business, and hope for the talented people in our business whose top skills are not necessarily people. We have to keep on growing and figure out our way, of course. Kay drew a map."

— **Mark L. Vincent,** PhD, EPC, CCNL,
Executive Advisor, Author, *Listening, Helping, Learning*

"What's your relationship code? How do you build relationships that last a lifetime and will be mutually beneficial? How do you honor and celebrate people? Kay Edwards has crafted a strong work that will help you craft answers to those questions. You'll discover a way to forge deeper long-term relationships with the people you meet on your life journey and your life will be all the richer for it."

— **Greg Leith,** Chief Executive Officer, Convene

"We were created as beings who need relationships, both personally and professionally. This book takes the mystery out of building lasting business relationships. And it proves that anyone can get better at networking and creating a culture of relationship-building in their organization. It takes the ick factor out of networking and shows why it's important for everyone to have a relationship code and put it into practice. There are so many practical tips and applications that anyone can adopt. I highly recommend it for leaders, entrepreneurs, consultants, *my students,* or anyone who wants to expand their network of trusted business relationships."

— **Steve Board,** Professor, School of Business, Maranatha Baptist University

"People are created to be in relationship with each other but for busy executives networking with others can get pushed aside. In *Hunt With Your Pack* Kay Edwards gives real world advice on how to network whether you're a busy introvert, extrovert or anywhere in between."

— **Mike Tenpas,** CEO, UFS

"I hate networking. Which may explain why I love this book. *Hunt With Your Pack* pretty much wiped out all my excuses for not networking. Not by showing me how easy it is to network, though that was part of it. But by showing me why it matters so much and how most of my preconceived negative ideas of reaching out to others, particularly strangers or near strangers, were wrong. Now I can't say that I have become a lot better at keeping up with friends and colleagues. But I am trying or, as the book notes, I'm being more intentional. And the funny thing is that the rewards vastly outweigh the effort. My only regret is that I didn't have *Hunt With Your Pack* twenty years ago. I'm just grateful that Kay Edwards has written such a refreshing, encouraging, and practical guide to valuing relationships now for introverts like me who can gain so much from this timely topic."

— **Steve Brock,** Executive Producer, Brand:Wallop,
Author, *Meaningful Travel* and *The Creative Wild*

"We move towards success in life and business at the speed of relationships. Kay Edwards' new book, *Hunt With Your Pack* is an accelerator to build a better network and a way to create a lasting relationship legacy that will benefit the next generation of leaders."

— **Bishop Walter Harvey,**
Apostolic Leader|Embassy Center MKE
President|National Black Fellowship
WI+H Movement
Executive Director|PRISM EDC

"What's possible when you think about what gives life and vitality to your network? Answer: anything and everything. In *Hunt With Your Pack,* Kay Edwards sees building relationships as a nourishing, joyful, service-first orientation grounded in true authenticity. She has given this topic more and deeper thinking than nearly all of us…and now this is her gift to each of us."

— **Gary Hubbell,** Gary Hubbell Consulting

"Early in my career, I asked someone I admired for their network of so many friends, 'How do you do it? Do you have a system?' This was before PCs and smartphones. I imagined he had pages of names with notes and dates. He said, 'No, I just think of somebody and call them.' This is what a consultant friend of mine calls an 'unconscious competent.' They do something well, but they can't tell you how to do it. Kay Edwards is conscious and competent. She knows how to network and build friendships and tells you how to do it. Read this book, and you can do it, too."

— **Steve Woodworth,** CEO, Masterworks, Author, *Lost in Transition*

"As someone who's spent much of his career on the path of servant leadership, I find *Hunt With Your Pack* by Kay Edwards hits home. This isn't just another networking book—it's a powerful guide for leaders who want to build genuine, meaningful relationships that stand the test of time.

"Kay's approach is refreshingly different. She introduces the "relationship code," which, in my opinion, is a game-changer for anyone who believes that leadership is more than just making connections—it's about creating lasting, value-driven relationships. This book helps you think strategically about how to build a culture where relationships matter at every level of your organization.

"What I love most is how *Hunt With Your Pack* emphasizes leaving a legacy. It's not just about what you achieve during your time as a leader but about the relationships you build that continue to grow and flourish long after you're gone. It's a call to lead with intention, to put people first, and to make every connection count, inspiring us to invest in our relationships.

"If you're on a journey of servant leadership like I am, this book's lessons make it a 'must-read.' It's full of wisdom and practical advice that will help you build a network of relationships that truly last, making a real impact on your organization and beyond."

— **Gene A. Wright,** Assistant Professor,
MSOE Rader School of Business

HUNT
WITH
YOUR
PACK

HUNT
WITH
YOUR
PACK

Why Networking Alone Isn't Enough

KAY EDWARDS

ILLUMIFY
MEDIA.COM

Published by
Illumify Media Global
www.IllumifyMedia.com
"Let's bring your book to life!"

Library of Congress Control Number: 2024922481

Paperback ISBN: 978-1-959099-10-9

Typeset by Art Innovations (http://artinnovations.in/)
Cover design by Debbie Lewis

Printed in the United States of America

To my darling Don,
who helped me launch this journey.
Now you have all of eternity to make new friends.
I miss you.

CONTENTS

INTRODUCTION

Wke live in a lonely world. We live in a culture that values individual effort, the lone hero who saves the day, the genius who isolates himself in the ivory tower, trying to find a solution to the world's problems.

As I sit and write this introduction, I can see my neighbor's yard, which is full of thistles. They have finished blooming, a beautiful, purple-colored bloom. Never mind that we all consider them to be weeds. They are truly beautiful. And now the blooms have turned to seed. It is a lovely summer day, and the west wind is carrying the seeds from these thistles across the neighborhood. The air is thick with them. They are landing in my yard, my neighbor's yard, and the yard next to hers. There is no stopping them. Next spring we will wonder where all of those thistles came from. And some of us will remember this day, this wind, this single patch of thistles that sprouted an army.

Relationships are like the wind that carries the seeds of ideas, innovation, and progress. Of course, we learn from data, from information organized into books and videos. But I have found that the ideas that take root, that travel the farthest and have the most impact, are the ones that are carried by relationships.

In *The Quiet Before: On the Unexpected Origins of Radical Ideas*, Gal Beckerman chronicles the origins of ten movements, the first happening in 1635, that all began with relationships. Most of them long before the invention of social media. In the book's introduction he says, "We are gripped by the moment when the crowd coalesces on the street—the adrenaline, the tear gas, the deafening chants, a policeman on horseback chasing down a lone protester or a man standing up to a tank. But if we rewind to the instant when a solid block of shared reality is first cracked, it's usually a group of people talking."[1]

We all understand the concept of networking. There are far too many books about networking that explain how to use relationships to get a job, to make a sale, or to get ahead in one's industry. This is not one of those books. This is also not a self-help book for introverts to improve their networking skills. There is a lot of help in this book for those who don't think they are very good at networking, but that is not what this book focuses on.

This book is about why we build relationships in the first place. What the role of relationship building is in an enterprise, and how to do it more intentionally so that we can reap the benefits of our relationship investments, just like we reap the benefits of our financial investments. If you are good at building business relationships, this book is for you because it will help you become more intentional about what comes naturally to you. It will also help you convey that knowledge to those on your team who may be struggling with relationship building.

If you are not so good at building business relationships but are willing to practice, this book will give you the tools to help you improve. Not everyone will turn into a master networker, but everyone can get better by understanding and practicing the building blocks of good relationships. I promise.

Hunt with Your Pack is the culmination of my thirty-five years of building business relationships to support my consulting practice. Most of us like to think that leaders hire us for our skills and experience, and I think that is mostly true. We would never have repeat business without those. But at the end of the day, the best consulting engagements are the ones in which my skills and experience are the right fit for the client's challenge, the client is someone I enjoy working with, and they enjoy working with me. A good relationship plus the right skills equals a successful engagement.

I have spent my career helping leaders learn more about their organizations, their constituents, and their markets through a variety of market research and listening strategies.

There is a heuristic used by many market research professionals that outlines the path from data to wisdom known as DIKW, sometimes called the information pyramid. This framework describes how we arrive at wisdom by beginning with data and transforming it through multiple stages: D = Data, I = Information, K = Knowledge, and W = Wisdom. Many experts think that the idea of the DIKW relationship originated from two lines in the poem: "Choruses" by T. S. Eliot that appears in the pageant play *The Rock* in 1934:

Where is the wisdom we have lost in knowledge?

Where is the knowledge we have lost in information?[2]

Others credit the musician Frank Zappa, based on the following quote.

Information is not knowledge.

Knowledge is not wisdom.

Wisdom is not truth.

Truth is not beauty.

Beauty is not love.

Love is not music.

Music is THE BEST.[3]

At Outsight Network, this framework has driven much of our thinking about how to create value for our clients based on the data we collect for them. The following illustration shows the progression from data to wisdom and how we move our clients from simply giving them data to helping them make wise decisions.

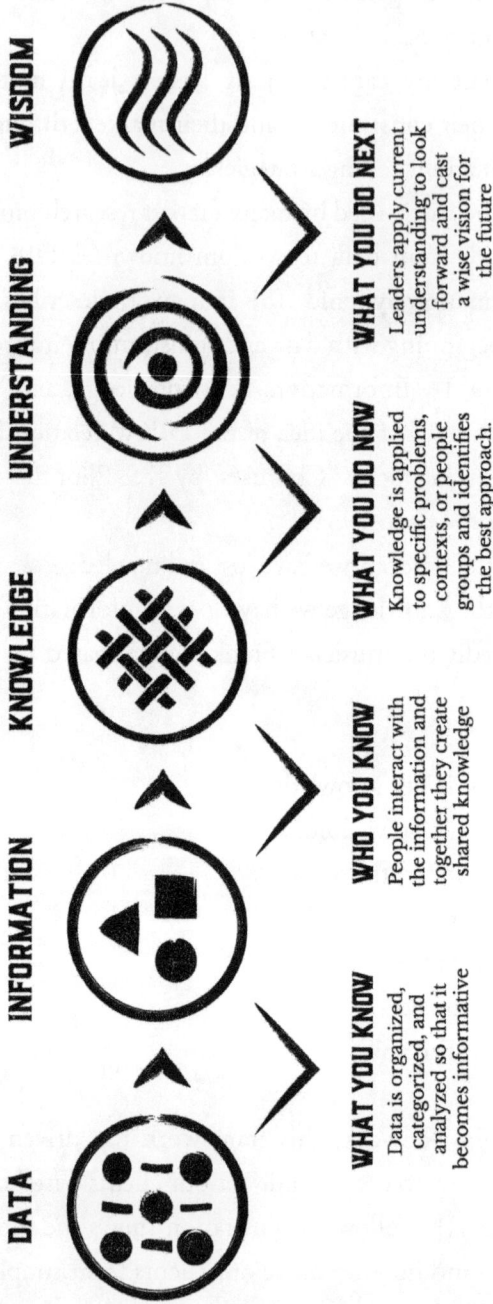

DATA → **INFORMATION** → **KNOWLEDGE** → **UNDERSTANDING** → **WISDOM**

WHAT YOU KNOW
Data is organized, categorized, and analyzed so that it becomes informative

WHO YOU KNOW
People interact with the information and together they create shared knowledge

WHAT YOU DO NOW
Knowledge is applied to specific problems, contexts, or people groups and identifies the best approach.

WHAT YOU DO NEXT
Leaders apply current understanding to look forward and cast a wise vision for the future

This figure shows the progression from data to wisdom, and the processes that need to take place to move from one stage to another. We believe there are four key components that every organization needs to make wise forward-moving decisions:

1. The right data (what you know)
2. The right people (who you know)
3. The right application (what you do now)
4. The right discernment (what you do next)

There are many books that can show you how to collect the right data in the appropriate ways to reduce bias and make sure you are getting accurate information. There are many professional researchers who can do that work for you. But this book is about having the right *people* around you. I'm not only referring to your employee team, but to the people far beyond your team, even beyond your industry, so that you can create the knowledge you need to carry you into a successful future.

HOW TO USE THIS BOOK

I have purposely kept this book brief and to the point in hopes that you read it in its entirety. It is organized into sections, so you can skip around and start wherever works best for you. In every section there are bullet points, lists, and fun exercises to help access the content quickly and easily.

SECTION ONE: CHAPTERS 1–5

This section introduces the concept of a "Relationship Code," which is your unique approach to building business relationships. It explains why having a Relationship Code is important for business leaders and senior teams and includes numerous diagnostics to help you identify what approach is best for you and your organization.

SECTION TWO: CHAPTERS 6–13

This chapter outlines the steps for creating a Relationship Code, determining your own relationship value code, and putting it all into practice in your professional life. Be sure to go to (kayedwardsauthor. com) to download the templates you will need to create a Relationship Code that works for you.

SECTION THREE: CHAPTERS 14–15

The final section of the book is especially relevant for senior teams who want to put an effective Relationship Code to work in their organization. It will also benefit leaders in the last third of their leadership journey who want to leave a relationship legacy for the next generation.

This book is for two kinds of people: those who are already building a business network and those who haven't started yet because they think they don't know how. Notice I said, "think they don't know how." Anyone can do a better job of building business relationships, and it has nothing to do with being born a networker.

For those who are already at the top of the networking game, this book will help you understand what you do well so that you can embed it in your whole organization, so that you are not the one "lonely one at the top," doing all the networking.

For those who think they don't know how to network, this book will help you develop your own unique road map to relationship-building success. Everyone truly is different, and I am not going to tell you what will work for you. Instead, I will guide you through a process that anyone can apply, no matter where you are on the networking spectrum, that will get you further than you ever thought possible.

Will the process in this book turn everyone into a master networker? Probably not. But everyone who starts out on the journey will make progress. Everyone who consistently applies at least some of these practices will find that everything is a little easier. As you develop more relationships, you will learn what works for you and what doesn't.

LEARNING FROM
RELATIONSHIP GIANTS

Early in the process of writing this book, I reached out to one of the best networkers I know and asked if I could interview him as part of my research. My goal was to learn from the best and test my approach with someone who seemed, at least from my observation, to make relationship connections effortlessly. I also used what researchers call a "snowball technique." At the end of the interview, I asked my interviewee to introduce me to the one person he thought of as the best networker he knows. That led me to my next interviewee, and to the next, and so on.

Through this process I interviewed ten individuals who have achieved stunning success in their careers, and who credit their network of business relationships with contributing significantly to their success. While everyone I interviewed describes themselves as someone for whom networking comes easily, they also all approach the practice with a great deal of intentionality and care. In other words, they bring their personal integrity and values to the process of building business relationships, and they practice what they preach. They took the time to answer my questions thoughtfully and thoroughly and shared openly about what worked for them and what didn't, even though I was a stranger to them. I experienced each person I interviewed as generous, humble, gracious, open, and genuine, which lends credibility to their networking approach. If it works for them, it can work for others too.

A set of common themes emerged from these interviews that help to add color and richness to the practice of networking. Throughout the book, I will call out these themes and share the voices of these networking giants with you.

In his beautiful book *The Great Divorce*, C. S. Lewis described hell as a place where people are constantly moving away from each other, where those who have been there the longest have the fewest relationships.[4] If that is the definition of hell, then it should be our goal to build lasting relationships here and in the hereafter.

Whether or not you believe in the hereafter, my greatest hope is that this book leads to deeper relationships for you and your business. May the relationships you foster bring you joy, both personally and professionally.

CHAPTER 1

THE BUSY LEADER'S NETWORKING DILEMMA

You're busy. Everyone's busy. We compete to be the busiest person we know. We wear our busyness like a badge of honor. I get it. Maybe you are too busy to network, especially if you are not sure why you are meeting with someone, or what they can do for you. It's best to leave networking to the salespeople. That's what you pay them for, right? Or maybe you are the one who is so busy with meetings and sales calls that you never really stop and think about how to make use of all the relationship capital that you are building.

Whether you hate networking and shy away from it, or whether you are doing it all the time because it comes easily for you, busyness gets in the way of building great business relationships.

I have a friend who I will call Dan. Dan is the CEO of a small manufacturing business. He is a great leader, and his employees love him. He is smart, he is a good businessman, he cares deeply for his employees, and he runs his company with a great sense of integrity, always thinking about how he can benefit his employees, his customers, and his community through his business.

But . . . Dan hates to network. He is an engineer by training, and he is at his best when he is behind his computer, working on spreadsheets, thinking about the numbers that run his business. While he is very personable and pleasant to be with (everyone loves Dan), he believes networking is something he can delegate to his salespeople.

As a result, Dan is always too busy to reach beyond his immediate circle of employees, a few select customers, and company suppliers. For him, busyness is a barrier to relationship building, and that's okay for him because it is something he doesn't want to do.

I have another friend, Kathy. Kathy loves to network. She attends breakfast meetings most mornings and spends many evenings at dinners, events, and customer meetings. She knows her business depends on having a large circle of relationships in her community with business leaders, nonprofit leaders, and almost anyone else she can connect with. She gets her energy from networking, and it comes naturally for her.

The challenge for Kathy is that her networking style creates too much busyness in her life, even though it creates business for her firm. When I ask her how she manages her relationships or how she is growing her relationship capital through all these meetings, she doesn't have an answer.

Her style of networking means that she has little opportunity to pause and think about how she can be more intentional with her business relationships to propel her business forward. For her, it is a game of quantity over quality.

Relationship capital, according to Wikipedia, is "the value inherent in a company's relationships with its customers, vendors, and other important constituencies. It also includes knowledge, capabilities, procedures, and systems which are developed from relationships with external agents."[1] Just like financial capital, we can benefit from the knowledge of others outside of our organization.

How much can we benefit? According to Metcalf's Law, the value of a network is proportional to the square of the number of connected members of the network.[2] That means the value of our network does not grow by addition; it grows exponentially. However, more relationships do not always yield real relationship capital. There is a human limit to our capacity to maintain helpful relationships. Economist Rod Beckstrom theorizes that "the value of a network equals the net value added to each user's transactions conducted through that network, summed over all users."[3] In other words, there is a point of diminishing returns in any network where the resources of the network are not enough to support new members. Like Goldilocks, our networking strategy should not be too little or too much. Rather, it must be intentional enough so that everyone in the network can benefit.

What makes a networking strategy intentional? The definition of *intentional*, according to Merriam Webster, is something that is "done by intention or design."[4] An intentional networking strategy is something that you deliberately plan for, set goals for, spend time on, and then measure the results. It considers the latest research on how humans build and maintain relationships, and it puts the other person and their needs at the center of the relationship.

Anything that we do with intentionality is more likely to be more effective than the things we leave to chance. Business relationships are no different. Please know that I am not advocating for turning your relationship practice into a soulless checklist of things to do. I am saying that when we pay attention to others, put their needs at the center of the relationship, and develop habits that keep those relationships strong, everyone will benefit.

How intentional are your current relationship-building habits? Take the following quiz to find out.

QUIZ: HOW INTENTIONAL IS YOUR RELATIONSHIP BUILDING?

For each of the following statements, think about how well it describes you. If five points means the statement describes you completely, and one point means the statement does not describe you at all, for each statement give yourself a score based on your current relationship-building practices.

1. I have a plan for what types of stakeholders I will meet with every month, including the total number of meetings with each.
2. I frequently reach out to people to set meetings rather than wait for others to contact me.
3. I take time before every meeting to identify an objective.
4. I always ask new people I meet to do something small for me.
5. I leave every meeting knowing what I will do next with or for the person I have met with.
6. I always follow up with what I promised to do in a meeting.
7. If I haven't seen someone in more than a year, I still know the best strategy to connect with them.
8. I leave space in my calendar to meet with new people who contact me, even if I don't know how they can help me.
9. I frequently connect people I meet to others in my network.
10. I have a specific set of reasons for ending a business relationship, and I take steps to manage that process.

Now add up your points. How did you do? If you scored more than 38 points, you are an intentional relationship-building star, and hopefully you are mentoring others on your team to be able to do the same.

If you scored fewer than 12 points, there is some work to be done on the intentionality of your relationship building. But there is no reason to despair. Few of us have ever been taught how to do this, and anyone can learn the specific practices that will help to build more sustainable relationship capital.

In the 1990s British anthropologist Dr. Robin Dunbar suggested that humans can only maintain 150 stable relationships at a single time. He devised this theory based on his study of primates' social interactions and extrapolating his results based on the size of human brains. Dunbar explained it informally as "the number of people you would not feel embarrassed about joining uninvited for a drink if you happened to bump into them in a bar."[5] Known as Dunbar's Number, these 150 relationships include *all* our relationships: our family members, our neighbors, our friends at church, our coworkers, and professional acquaintances outside of our companies.

Whether you agree with his methodology or not, the idea has grown popular enough that some businesses have even organized divisions and office facilities so that no more than 150 people work in the same location. Churches seldom grow beyond 150 members with a single pastor.

There are several challenges that these research data present for those who are trying to grow their relationship capital. First, because this number includes all our relationships, both personal and professional, it challenges us to make the most of the relationships we are currently in. This suggests a level of intentionality that most people don't apply to their relationships. How often do you sit down and think about your 150 closest relationships and how they contribute to your professional success?

Second, it challenges us to find creative ways to expand beyond the number, especially if we are responsible for business development, or lead a larger organization for which 150 relationships will never be enough to ensure the sustainability of the business.

Third, it forces us to think about why, when, and how to end relationships that are no longer healthy or mutually beneficial. Most of us are too busy getting through our days to bring this level of intentionality to our relationship management process.

So how do we introduce this level of intentionality when we can barely get through our email inbox and our endless to-do lists? I have found that the first step is to practice on a few relationships. Intentional relationship building is like a muscle that few of us realize we need to exercise, but once we start, it gets easier. The following challenge will help you get that relationship-building muscle moving.

CHALLENGE: CREATE A RELATIONSHIP MAP

Step One: List your five closest business relationships. For the purposes of this exercise, it doesn't matter what their role is or how you are connected to them. It is up to you to decide what "close" means to you.

Step Two: For each person in your relationship map, answer the following questions:
- How did you meet them?
- What is their greatest strength?
- What do you rely on them to do for you?
- What do they rely on you to do for them?
- Who is one person they could introduce you to who would be beneficial to your business?

Step Three: Think about your answers to those questions. Are there any patterns you see emerging? Are there questions you did not know the answers to? Did any of the answers make you uncomfortable? For example, do your closest relationships come from the same sources? Do they bring the same strengths to the table? Are there strengths missing that you really need? Do you struggle to know what you can offer in a relationship? Do you find it difficult to identify who they could introduce you to, and why? Have any of the relationships changed in any way, good or bad, in the last year or so?

As you review your relationship map, it may be that you feel some discomfort with one or more of the questions you asked yourself about each relationship. For example, many of us are uncomfortable with the idea that we rely on others to do something for us. That is not uncommon, and it is related to the myths or misperceptions we often carry regarding what we typically think of as networking.

Most often there are three types of discomfort or unease about the idea of business networking or relationship building:

1. Leveraging
2. Multiplying
3. Ending

LEVERAGING

Most of us are uncomfortable with the thought of "using" other people to get what we want. It is one of the reasons that networking can sometimes feel manipulative or unsavory, especially for those of us who consider ourselves to be introverts. Conventional wisdom about networking says that to avoid this discomfort, we must first do someone a favor, then they will be obligated to us to return that favor. In his book *Give and Take*, Adam Grant identifies three different personality types: Givers, Takers, and Matchers. Matchers, according to Grant, are most likely to feel this discomfort because they are the most likely to take a transactional approach to relationship building. And while Givers are more likely, by nature, to do someone else a favor, they are also least likely to expect anything in return.[6] According to research by Shalom H. Schwartz and Anat Bardi, most individuals in the United States (and in eleven other countries) rate giving as their single most important value.[7]

So we are left between a rock and a hard place, knowing that others have strengths and assets that would be beneficial to us, but not knowing how to ask them for help without feeling manipulative.

The answer to this dilemma is to remember that our human brains are wired to find pleasure in helping others. The person on the other end of your business relationship wants to help. This is often called the Benjamin Franklin Effect because of a story in his autobiography in which Franklin describes how he won over a political rival. Franklin wrote to his rival and asked to borrow a rare book that the rival had in his library. The rival agreed, and a week later Franklin returned the book with a letter expressing how much he liked it. Over time, the two men became great friends. Franklin said, "He that has once done you a kindness will be more ready to do you another, than he whom you yourself have obliged."[8]

Remembering that people generally like to help can overcome the idea that leveraging our relationships is manipulative or underhanded. Yes, it can turn into that if we act out of selfish motives and don't put the other person in the center of the relationships. But we can give people an opportunity to help us by asking them to engage in a relationship that allows them to bring their strengths and skills to the table for the benefit of everyone.

MULTIPLYING

Shouldn't we be happy with the relationships we have? Grateful for the people God has put in our lives? Isn't it wrong to look at our relationships as a stepping stone to who they know? We have all been in conversations at networking events where the person we are speaking with keeps looking over our shoulder to see if there is someone more important in the room. We never want to be that person, so why would we ask people we know to introduce us to someone in their network? That just feels icky.

The answer to this discomfort also lies in our wiring as human beings, and our interconnectedness. We are designed to be in relationship, and what impacts one of us in a social network impacts everyone in that network. Humans share a universal longing to be known and to be loved. When someone in our network connects us to someone else, it makes the network stronger and more cohesive, which benefits everyone.

In *The Book of Forgiving*, Bishop Desmond Tutu makes the case that this interconnectedness is described through the concept of Ubuntu, which means, "humanity." "It is the philosophy and belief that a person is only a person through other people. In other words, we are human only in relation to other humans. Our humanity is bound up in one another, and any tear in the fabric of connection between us must be repaired for us all to be made whole. This interconnectedness is the very root of who we are."[9]

The statistical science of social network analysis confirms this. Sociologists and others use social network analysis to measure the strength of a network—for example, a classroom of students, employees of an organization, or members of an association. This science measures the strength of connections or "ties" between individuals and uses this information to identify who the thought leaders in the network are. The strength of a tie between two people is the combination of the amount of time, the emotional intensity, the intimacy, and the reciprocal services that are involved in the relationship. People with strong ties tend to be more similar to one another.

However, according to research conducted by Mark S. Granovetter published in the *American Journal of Sociology* in 1973, innovation tends to travel more effectively between people with weak ties rather than strong, possibly because those with strong ties are so similar. He discovered that those searching for employment most often heard about openings through weak ties, such as people who were acquaintances rather than close friends. He concluded that, "Individuals with many weak ties are best placed to diffuse innovation."[10] Weak ties reach a greater number of people through shorter pathways than strong ties.

Multiplying our networks by asking others for introductions and creating more mutual connections helps to strengthen your network and that of the person you are asking to make the introduction.

ENDING

If, when looking at your relationship map, you realized that some of your relationships might not be as close now as they have been, you may have felt some discomfort about that. It is hard to face that every one of our relationships will end at some point, whether we want them to or not. Sometimes they end because someone has died, which brings terrible grief and loss into our lives. Sometimes they end because situations change and people we were once close to by circumstance simply aren't around as often as they used to be, and that can bring a deep feeling of loss as well. And sometimes we choose to end relationships because they are no longer healthy and life-giving, and that is hard too.

In business relationships, we tend to let relationships fade away, especially when circumstances change. At Outsight Network, our average client engagement is between four and twelve months long. We do great work. We are fully engaged with our clients, addressing their opportunities and challenges. We develop relational bonds that help our teams perform well and make our clients successful. And then we go away.

I have experienced two ends of an emotional spectrum at the end of client engagements. I can feel like I am standing at the door of my client's office with my nose pressed up against the glass saying, "Remember me? Remember how good that was?" Or, I can't wait to be done with the project, shaking the dust off my feet in frustration at the end of the engagement. Sure, I did good work, but it was hard, and something about the relationship wasn't right. Instead of sticking around to fix it, it can be so much easier to just walk away.

Ending a business relationship should be something that we do intentionally, the right way, for the right reasons. What are the right reasons to end a relationship? According to author Dr. Henry Cloud, we can "set limits on our own exposure to people who are behaving poorly; we can't change them or make them behave right. Our model is God. He does not really 'set limits' on people to 'make them' behave. God sets standards, but he lets people be who they are and then separates himself from them when they misbehave."[11] It's okay to intentionally end a relationship that is harmful or one-sided.

Just like talking about money, I think that most of us are uncomfortable with an intentional process of ending relationships. It's hard. It forces us to experience loss. It sometimes requires us to have difficult conversations. So, we let it just happen rather than create an intentional process around it.

In *Fierce Conversations*, author Susan Scott suggests that part of a leader's role is to take responsibility for his or her emotional wake. This means that we need to understand how our role as leaders impacts those around us. And when it is time to end a relationship, we need to take responsibility for doing it well.

"If you created a mess, either single-handedly or in partnership with someone, do not bolt when things get emotional. Some topics of conversation are dicey, at best. But if you started it or you caused it, stay to the finish, even if the finish isn't what you had envisioned ahead of time. You hoped for twittering bluebirds. You ended up with a seriously teed off condor. Sit. Stay. Complete. Sometimes you just need a well-oiled reverse gear."[12]

Whether it is a difficult conversation or not, intentionally ending a business relationship that is no longer valuable to both parties is the kind thing to do. That means we need to have a carefully thought-through set of reasons why we might end a relationship and a process for ending it well. That list will be different for every individual and every firm. To be clear, not every relationship needs to end, even relationships that have gone dormant for many years.

The answer to the busy person's networking dilemma is to understand the power of intentionality as we go about building and maintaining our relationships. It takes the understanding that we are finite human beings with our own networking styles and limitations. Most individuals can't maintain enough relationships to grow and sustain a business. This means that in addition to your personal Relationship Code, you need an approach, a Relationship Code that leverages the strengths of those around you. Even if you are a solopreneur, you likely have professional colleagues and others around you who care about the success of your business. They are a part of your team. Relationship building is something that that anyone can get better at with practice. It requires a great networking code that leverages, multiplies, and ends with integrity, celebrates our human wiring, puts aside all selfishness, and honors our God-given need to know and be known.

KEY TAKEAWAYS

- We need relationships with a growing network of people to grow and sustain our businesses.
- Whether you are a natural networker, or someone who is more hesitant about networking, building intentionality into your networking practice will benefit you, your business, and everyone you meet.
- Our human limitations mean that we need to approach networking as a team effort.
- Leveraging, multiplying, and ending relationships when we need to honors the way we were created and invites others to live out their God-given purpose as well.

CHAPTER 2

WHY THERE ARE NO GO-AWAY RELATIONSHIPS

A s you created the list of your five closest relationships in the previous chapter, you may have noticed some relationships cross the line between business and personal. But there really is no such thing as a line between business and personal relationships. Family members, people you see at church and community events, your neighbors—really anyone you meet—come with their own network of relationships. The line between personal and professional is arbitrary. It is an artificial construct that we hide behind. Maybe we hide behind it because we are uncomfortable with the concept of "networking" as most people understand it.

What makes us uncomfortable with thinking about our relationships in a comprehensive, non-siloed way? Sometimes we are afraid that mixing business and personal relationships will "foul the waters." What if something goes wrong in our business relationships? We can always walk away from those, right? Those are temporary. We do business and then go home to our families. If things go wrong, we never really have to interact with that person again. We can end the contract with the client. We can fire the recalcitrant employee. We can stop showing up at the networking events run by the person we don't like. We can hide behind an artificial label of "business relationship."

What if God never intended for us to draw those artificial lines in our relationships? I happen to be convinced by my faith in God that each person is an eternal being, a precious soul who deserves to be treated with dignity. There is no one who is temporary or unimportant.

If this is true, that we are all important, then there are lasting implications for the way I treat business relationships. If everyone I meet is created by God to be an eternal being, there is no such thing as a go-away relationship. There is no one who matters only temporarily. There is no one I can treat as if what I do today doesn't have eternal consequences.

What does that mean from a practical, business perspective? It means that I need to treat every business relationship as if I may be spending eternity with that person. It doesn't mean that I make myself a doormat. It does mean that I treat everyone with integrity in the way that I would want to be treated. It means that I speak honestly. I do my best to live up to my promises. I don't cut corners, even if no one would notice. I lovingly confront any injustices I see whether they are toward me or toward someone else. Viewing every relationship as if it is eternal puts a hard line on every relationship. It sets a different kind of standard than we otherwise might put on our business relationships.

I have worked my whole career in go-away professions. I began in advertising. My first boss used to say that client relationships were like marriages. After seven years with an agency, a client starts to get itchy and wonder what else is out there. He cautioned that this is the time that an agency needs to pay special attention to the client to make sure they are happy with the work and the relationship. That was over thirty years ago. Now my colleagues in the agency world tell me that the average business relationship seems to last about one to two years. How can those of us who work in go-away professions treat our business relationships as something other than short-term? It is a question that I will ask you to grapple with as you develop your own Relationship Code throughout this book.

From advertising, I moved on to a firm that did capital campaign consulting. There, the average client engagement, or the length of a capital campaign, was about three years. Consultants in my firm often spent the majority of that time in the client's office, or meeting with their donors in their homes or businesses. It was an intense relationship for the three-year period of the campaign. We sometimes worried about consultants "going native" (becoming so much a part of the client's culture that they lost their objectivity and their ability to see the client's challenges from an outside perspective). But at the end of the campaign, the consultants and the clients parted ways. There was no reason for them to interact again until the next campaign, sometimes many years down the road.

Now, many nonprofit organizations are in a perpetual campaign and only engage consultants as outside advisors, not as embedded staff. In addition, the average tenure for a resource development professional is about eighteen months, according to the most recent study from the Association of Fundraising Professionals.

And now we are experiencing the "Great Resignation." According to the U.S. Bureau of Labor Statistics, the number of resignations reached an all-time high in 2021 since 2001, with almost forty-seven million people leaving their jobs voluntarily in 2021. All of this makes it too easy to think of our business relationships as transient, as things that we can easily shed if they don't go the way we want them to.

It reminds me of my trip to China with my graduate program. My classmates were eager to try their hand at shopping, particularly the act of negotiating. We cheered each other on to see who could get the best deals from the street vendors.

On one of the last days of the trip, I decided to buy a dress that caught my eye. It was the last opportunity to shop, and I was determined to flex my negotiating skills. I think getting a good deal on the dress was even more important to me than the dress was, having seen what my classmates had done. I wanted to prove to myself that I could negotiate a good deal as well.

After some serious back and forth with the vendor, he finally agreed to sell me the dress for the price I wanted. However, he was clearly frustrated with the process and thought I was being unreasonable. He agreed to the price and then declared, "I am done with you." In my mind, I was relieved. Not only had I acquired the dress at a good price, but I was done with the vendor as well, knowing that I would likely never see him again. So I gladly walked away.

If we are truly eternal beings, then in heaven there are no go-away relationships. In *The Great Divorce*, C.S. Lewis portrays heaven as the place where we must come to terms with our earthly relationships, no matter how painful. We have all of eternity to work on them.

In contrast, hell is described by one of the characters in the book as a place where people constantly move away from each other. "As soon as anyone arrives he settles in some street. Before he's been there twenty-four hours he quarrels with his neighbor. Before the week is over he's quarreled so badly that he decides to move. Very like he finds the next street empty because all the people there have quarreled with *their* neighbors—and moved."[1]

This does not mean that we stay in relationships that are abusive. Boundaries are healthy, and sometimes we need to move on from relationships that are harmful. We must love each other enough to confront injustice. We have the choice of renewing the relationship if the other person is willing to change their behaviors, or we can leave the relationship if they choose not to.

When my father was dying, this man who had been incredibly silent and stoic all his life suddenly became chatty, telling stories, sharing advice, saying things to us that he never would have said before. One day I asked him if he was looking forward to seeing his brothers and sisters in heaven. He was the youngest of six, and all his siblings had passed away. I expected him to say that he missed them, that he was looking forward to seeing them. I remembered that we had spent a lot of time with them when I was young, visiting them on Sundays, spending holidays with them, inviting them over to swim in our pool during the summer.

No, he was not looking forward to seeing them at all. He said that when he was young, they had bullied him. I was surprised at the pain in his voice. "I suppose we'll have to get over that," he said, as if forgiveness was something about heaven that he was dreading. It was apparent that the past behavior of his older brothers and sisters still seemed to hold power over him. His was a family that never said anything confrontational to each other. But he somehow knew that the confrontation was coming.

How do we reconcile heaven as a place where our spirits spend eternity, when we can't even get along with each other in our earthly bodies? Surely, we don't magically forget everything that happened here on earth when we get there. We are still ourselves. We are fearfully and wonderfully made, according to the book of Psalms. We are made in God's image, yet we are each created with fingerprints that are unique to us, with personalities that are unique to us. We do not leave those behind and become ghostly automatons when we enter eternity. I believe we enter eternity with our sense of self intact, including our memories, our strengths, and most importantly, our relationships. After all, the book of Hebrews says that we are surrounded by a glorious cloud of witnesses, many of whom the author called by name. When Jesus was transfigured, both Moses and Elijah were recognizable to the disciples and clearly had distinct personalities. They had not left their uniqueness behind them in their earthly bodies.

It's easy to say that this has implications for our personal and family relationships. That it's important to treat people as eternal beings if we are related to them, or go to church with them, or if they are our best friends. In most cases, those are the people we want to be with, and we would be sad if those relationships went away.

It's harder to think about our business relationships as eternal. Even on the surface, the implications of this are difficult. It means we must treat everyone with respect. We must tell the truth. We must confront injustice with grace. We must think about the impact our actions will have on others. We must put their needs at least equal with ours, if not ahead of ours. All things that are hard to do.

And what do eternal business relationships look like in a profession where the average client engagement is less than a year? How do we avoid treating our clients like a series of go-away relationships? Like the vendor in China shouting, "I am done with you!" when the project is over.

I have spent the past number of years thinking about this, defining what it means to bring an eternal perspective to business relationships. How do we create relationships with an eternal view? Relationships that we aren't dreading in eternity? Over time, I have created ways to stay in touch in ways that honor the relationship appropriately and puts the other person at the center of the relationship. This is the process I have outlined in this book, a way to develop your own unique Relationships Code.

In the opening chapter of this book, I spoke of the busy person's relationship dilemma. Some of us use our busyness to avoid networking. Others use our networking busyness to avoid bringing an appropriate intentionality to our networking activity. Both approaches leave us missing out on an enormous relationship potential.

Having an intentional and practical approach to networking will help you to treat all your relationships with eternal integrity. Wherever you are on the relationship spectrum, this approach will help you grow your network of relationships in a way that respects the eternal nature of others and the goal of building lasting relationships. For those of us who dislike the concept of networking and are hesitant about expanding our networks, this approach will encourage you to reach just far enough beyond your comfort zone to increase your relationship capital without being too scary or out of reach.

INVITE A HIGHER PURPOSE INTO THE PROCESS

Most of the relationship giants I spoke with have a personal faith in God and a daily practice of integrating their faith in their business activities, including their networking. This faith drives how they relate to people; for some, it also drives how they manage their networking time.

One interviewee cites the example of Jesus, saying that while Jesus ministered to the crowds, He spent the majority of His time pouring into a small group of disciples. This relationship giant says he manages his own time based on this model and has gone all-in on the people whom God has brought into his life, even if it is only a small group of people at any given time.

Others share similar strategies, saying that they trust God to help them manage their time and relationships wisely, including the number of relationships they focus on. These individuals say they count on God to work out their schedule. According to one interviewee, if you are following Christ and doing the things He has called you to do, He works out the schedule. This individual has experienced uncanny situations in which seemingly immovable work schedules have suddenly changed, allowing him to say yes to volunteer opportunities God has brought his way.

For those who are not instinctive networkers, I'm sure you have many questions. Where do I start? How do I reach out to new people? Who should I reach out to? Why would they want to talk with me? What's the best way to reach people? How often do I connect with them? Do I need to do them a favor before I ask them for something?

Those who network naturally ask a different set of questions. Where will I find more time to expand my network? Who can introduce me to the person that I want to meet? How can I keep track of everyone in my network? What can this person do for me?

The goal of intentionality can help both kinds of networkers accomplish more from their relationship-building efforts. Why do we build relationships? Because we are better together than we are separately. Because of all the reasons I listed in the opening chapter. Because of Dunbar's Number, which states we can only maintain 150 relationships at a time. It's impossible for any single entity or person to have all the resources they need to carry out their mission in the world. If God made us to be eternal beings, He also made us to be in community. He designed us to work better together.

Dunbar's Number, for those who *don't* like to network, means that we need to view all our relationships holistically, not just as friends or family members or business colleagues, but as a set of relationships who, in turn, have their own relationships. Whole people created in the image of a God who created us to be in community. It means that there is no separation between personal and business. God calls us to be in relationship and to work at expanding the reach of our relationships. Why? Because in doing so, we can be a blessing to others.

Dunbar's Number, for those of us who *love* to network, means that there are realistic limits to our individual reach. If we can only have 150 meaningful relationships at a time in our lives, how do we leverage the relationships we have to accomplish our personal and professional goals? It means that we need to bring a level of precision to our networking activity that we might not have thought about. It means we need to stop treating people as serial relationships and treat them as eternal. It means we need to make sure that we are treating everyone we meet with respect, regardless of who they are and what we think they can do for us.

Just like there are only so many hours in a day, there are only so many relationships we can manage. That means we need to make the most of our networking time.

For those who are born networkers, their connections can quickly become overwhelming and out of control. It is easy to lose track of why we are networking when we are overrun with requests for coffee meetings.

In 2014, Wendy McClelland—author, entrepreneur, and social media influencer—set off a firestorm on LinkedIn by saying she would no longer take coffee meetings. She determined they were a waste of time and kept her from pursuing other things that were more important. The article seemed to hit a nerve among readers, with commenters coming down on both sides of the coffee meeting debate. Some argued that there is value in meeting with anyone who asks, and that one never knows when serendipity will strike, when there will be unexpected connections and value from connecting. Others agreed that most of these requests are a waste of time, and too many people take up too much of one's time looking for free advice and asking for things with no intention to, or ability to, return the favor.[2]

I believe the truth lies somewhere in between these extremes. The lesson is that those who already have a large amount of relationship capital and large networks, or are in positions of significant influence, can be in a position where they need to manage their relationships carefully, and the limitations of Dunbar's Number requires them to be vigilant about overextending themselves.

The final dilemma for the busy networker is managing the information that is generated by all their networking activity. No matter how good you are at remembering names, faces, dates, and interesting personal facts, it will eventually all catch up with you. Frantic, you will find yourself searching your memory for some details about the person in front of you, when you met them, and what you talked about.

Politicians are famous for employing staff members who serve as their "people" memory, whispering names and facts into their ears as they meet the public. These individuals have often been portrayed as comedic caricatures in TV shows and movies. Most of us don't have the luxury of having a staff person to act as our exobrains as we move through our networking and relationship-building tasks. But if we don't keep track, we can quickly find ourselves in an awkward position.

Just like my early attempts at networking went awry because I had a flawed concept of what networking was and how to go about it, I learned, many times the hard way, that mindlessly collecting people without an intentional strategy can backfire as well.

I once sat at a coffee shop for half an hour, not realizing that the person I was supposed to meet was sitting twenty feet away from me. Neither one of us knew what the other person looked like, nor were we brave enough to search around the coffee shop looking for each other. (This was before the days of LinkedIn profile pictures.)

How many times have I asked people the same questions I had asked them in the meeting before? How many kids do you have? Do you play golf? Where did you go to school? How long have you been with the company? All of these are logical conversation topics, but only once. For someone who is meeting new people every week, it is too easy to fall back on these conversational conventions, and too easy to ask them at a second or third meeting, when you should already know the answer.

I have walked out of meetings countless times that were full of energy and connections and dropped the ball because I didn't take good notes on what we had agreed to do next. Or I forgot to make a connection I promised to make. Or I let too much time go by before I made the next connection.

Even now, I sometimes forget and go into meetings without identifying my goals, without reviewing my notes from the previous meeting with that person, and generally having no plan of action. Sometimes I can wing it. The other person is eager to connect, and we find that we have many areas of common interest. But that doesn't always happen so easily, and I have learned that the odds of a successful meeting are much higher when I prepare, when I know what I want to accomplish and I remember to focus on an outcome that will be beneficial for both me and the person I am meeting with.

All of these are the hazards of pushing the outer limits of networking activity, of being the busy networker trying to stretch the limits of Dunbar's Number. More importantly, they are signs that I need to remember that every person in front of me is an eternal being, created by and loved by an eternal God, and deserving of my attention.

KEY TAKEAWAYS

- There is no such thing as a business relationship or a personal relationship. There are just *relationships*. There is no artificial segmentation.

- We were all created by God as eternal beings, and each one of us is important simply because we exist.
- There are no go-away relationships. Everyone we meet is an eternal being, created and loved by God.
- We must intentionally choose how to manage our networking time because it is not possible for us to maintain more than 150 or so meaningful relationships at a given time.
- Wasting our relationship time is neither fair to us nor to the person we are networking with.

CHAPTER 3

WHY YOUR BUSINESS NEEDS A RELATIONSHIP CODE

L eading a business is like a poor imitation of junior high: The smartest kids don't always win. The popular kids pick the next cool trend so often that the rest of the kids can't keep up. Everyone feels a little bit awkward and unsure of themselves inside, even if they don't admit it. If you could just be a part of the "in" crowd, life would be so much easier.

That awkward feeling from junior high seems to have followed most of us into adulthood. A search for "networking" on Amazon yields more than sixty thousand books, including many aimed at introverts, nerds, and geeks. In other words, anyone who thinks they were on the wrong side of the junior high playground. Most of us probably have leftover feelings of not knowing how to break into the "in" crowd and use relationships to build our business success.

We have all heard this saying from a business perspective: "It's not what you know, it's who you know." Most of us can pinpoint those people who can effortlessly make connections and get what they need in life. We often wonder how to make and leverage connections that will help us move our businesses forward—whether we are the CEO of an enterprise, the leader of a senior team, or a solopreneur trying to build a profitable practice.

MY NETWORKING NIGHTMARE

My first experience with what I thought of as networking came early in my career, and it didn't go as well as I wanted it to. In fact, it was kind of a disaster. I had always heard about this thing called *networking*. I wanted to be one of those people who knew people and knew how to use relationships to get things done.

Now was my chance.

This was my first real job as a consultant, and I was leading prospect research services for the fundraising firm I worked for, which required me to gather as much information on donor prospects as I could using publicly available sources. Nonprofits rely on this kind of information when preparing to ask major donors for gifts. In turn, major donors expect nonprofits to do their homework and know their likes and giving interests before being asked for money.

I sat at my desk and looked at the phone, aware that this was the moment when I needed to network. I needed to call someone I had worked with who knew the prospect I was researching. It was a strange request to make of someone: "Tell me everything you know about X. I'm not being creepy or anything like that. I just hunt to know because one of my clients is about to meet with him, and I thought you might be able to share."

I couldn't say that, but I had written everything I wanted to say on a legal pad and kept it in front of me for when I made the call. I carefully and painstakingly practiced my script beforehand and thought of every eventuality. I had written different versions of the script so that nothing would surprise me.

When I had imagined and planned for everything, including how nice I was going to be and how the person on the other end would respond, I picked up the phone. Except, I hadn't thought of everything. At the end of the conversation, when I thanked him for his time, I said, "I owe you lunch." I thought that's what "networking" was all about. I thought that when I asked for something, I owed the other person something back.

"Why?" he asked?

Why? I couldn't think of an answer. My mind raced: *Because you gave me something? Because I bothered you in the middle of a workday? Because buying you lunch would be a good way to pay you back? Because I mistakenly thought that you would enjoy spending a lunch with me?*

My carefully concocted script went horribly awry at that moment. I stuttered a goodbye and hung up the phone. What had I missed? What had I done wrong? Why didn't that go the way I thought it would go?

Maybe I needed to rethink what I understood about networking.

This question has haunted me ever since: Why? Why would anyone want to connect with me? What value could I possibly add to this person? Go directly back to junior high. Do not pass go. Do not collect $200.

WHY YOUR BUSINESS NEEDS RELATIONSHIPS

Twenty-five years ago, when I first started in consulting, I spent hours of my week writing out everything I would say on every phone call. I had never learned how to talk with people. My parents were farmers. My older brothers became farmers. My older sisters became housewives. No one I knew picked up the phone and called someone to do business.

But if I wanted to do what I saw other successful consultants doing, I had to learn how to network. I had to learn how to sell myself and my services. I had to develop business relationships. I was good at doing things, at listening, and at organizing data. I was good at seeing patterns and creating structure, at observing people and understanding what they said, and creating solutions to their problems. But none of that involved building a relationship. What I didn't understand was that if I wanted to do those things for a living, I also had to be good at building trust, at getting people to trust me to do those things for them. At least enough so that they would open their checkbooks and pay me to help them.

Bob Burg, author of *Endless Referrals*, states, "People will do business with and refer business to those people they know, like and trust.[1] How could I, the world's biggest introvert, get people to like me enough to do business with me?

In the last chapter we learned that intentionality trumps both quality and quantity in business relationships. There are four reasons why leaders need to think intentionally about relationship building:

1. Trust
2. Risk
3. Attrition
4. Innovation

TRUST

In *The Speed of Trust* by Stephen R. Covey, he says that the speed of business is a function of trust, and that money flows faster in relationships where the trust level is high than it does in relationships where there is little trust. Therefore everything we do goes faster and runs more efficiently when we have strong business relationships.

"Once you really understand the hard measurable economics of trust, it's like putting on a new pair of glasses. Everywhere you look, you can see the impact—at work, at home, in every relationship, in every effort. You can begin to see the incredible difference high-trust relationships can make in every dimension of life."[2]

You need business relationships because trust is the currency of business. Your business needs relationships because everything is easier when we trust each other. People want to do business with people they like. Trust is what keeps people coming back, even when things don't go exactly like we expect them to.

I believe there are two types of people in the world: those who are already building great business relationships and those who aren't. The people who are building great business relationships do so instinctively. You know who they are. They have thousands of LinkedIn connections. They have a full calendar of networking meetings and sales meetings. They meet with people inside and outside of their industry. They enjoy making new connections. When they have a business need, they don't hesitate to reach out to someone who has the resources they need. Things work easily for them because they have a network. They always know who to contact and who to reach out to, and they always know the right person with the right resource at the right time. More importantly, people always seem to respond positively to them.

But when I ask them how they build their network, and what steps they take to maintain it, they often look at me with a puzzled expression. As one consummate networker said to me, "You just do it." For him, it all comes so easily and so effortlessly that he rarely stops to think about how he does it. He knows it is an important part of his leadership style, and important to the success of his business, but he doesn't really think about the components of his networking approach and how he implements each step. If he had to teach his process to someone else, he probably couldn't.

At the other end of the spectrum are people who don't "just do it" because the "it" is a big mystery; worse, it's a mental trip back to junior high. They had no role models, or even if they did, perhaps their role models didn't fully know how to break down what they do in a way that was teachable. This second group looks at networking and struggles to know where to start, how not to feel awkward, or how to unlock the mystery of what looks so easy for others. They struggle, honestly, with the *why*.

Many people go into a profession because they love what they do. Each of us is gifted with talents and abilities and experiences that no other person in the world has, and using those skills and abilities in our professions brings joy. It allows us to wake up every morning and love what we do. Personally, I love that moment when I am working with a client and together we create that aha moment when we begin to see everything clearly, when we can finally see the way forward through what was once confusing and complicated.

But to do that, I need people to trust me. I need them to know who I am and how my skills will benefit them and their organizations. If they are going to trust me enough to engage me to help their organizations, we must first have a relationship.

Every business owner and every senior leader needs to know how to build great relationships. Increasingly, we all want to do business with people we know and trust. To prove this point, think about your most profitable customer relationship. How did it start? What did it take to foster that relationship? What are you doing to maintain it?

How many of the following statements apply to that relationship?

- ☐ They will answer the phone when you call.
- ☐ They will refer you to someone they know.
- ☐ You don't mind doing them a favor.
- ☐ You can be honest with them when things go wrong in the business relationship.
- ☐ You trust them to do the right thing, even if it isn't written in a contract.
- ☐ They are willing to tell you when things need to improve.
- ☐ They seek you out first when they have a new business need.
- ☐ They ask your opinion on their highest-level business challenges.
- ☐ They engage you year after year for different kinds of projects.

☐ They will call you to ask for your advice.

☐ They will offer you ideas to help improve your business.

Now, ask those same questions about your least profitable customer. How many statements apply to that relationship?

RISK

My first volunteer board leadership role was for a small nonprofit organization. This organization worked in an urban area, and its mission was to bring peace to neighborhoods that are troubled by violence. Every Saturday in the summer months, this organization went into a city park and brought peace. They served a free lunch to anyone who showed up—sometimes as many as a thousand people. They held games and activities for the kids. They gave away toys. Most importantly, they brought a message of peace and love.

The most amazing thing about this organization was that all of this was done by an army of volunteers who lovingly showed up week after week because of the convictions of their faith and their belief that what they were doing was important. The entire organization was led by one full-time employee, the executive director, who sold sporting equipment as a side gig to make ends meet.

I had been on the board for a few months and had just taken over the role of board chair when I got a call on a Saturday morning saying the executive director had been killed in a car accident. He had fallen asleep at the wheel of his truck and had plowed into the back of a semi-truck that was stopped in front of him. His laptop, which had been on the seat of the truck beside him, was smashed, along with all of the pertinent information about the organization, its operations, and, most importantly, all of the executive director's contacts.

This was a man who knew instinctively how to network. He was a natural relationship builder, and he used this strength to grow his business and the work of the nonprofit. He was the one who inspired the army of volunteers who carried out the mission of peace week in and week out. He was the one everyone rallied around, including all the board members. At his funeral, it took almost two hours to get through the line of people who stood up to say a few words of tribute to him.

Why is this an important story to remember? Because when this man died, all his relationship capital died with him. We had all relied on him to make things happen through his networking ability. When we lost that, it took significant effort to rebuild the organization and its mission in the city.

Fortunately for me, a few key volunteers stepped in to keep the organization going. One of them was blessed with the same kind of natural relationship-building skills that the former executive director had, and he stepped into the role of executive director and carried on the work of the organization.

The point of this story is that this organization had no relational plan in place, no way to mitigate the risk of losing a key leader and his relationship capital in one catastrophic event. How many other organizations are living with this kind of risk?

The following questions will give you a quick tally of the relationship risk in your organization.

RELATIONSHIP RISK QUIZ

On a scale of 1 to 5, with 5 being "Describes Completely," and 1 being "Does Not Describe at All," how well do each of the following statements describe your organization?

- ☐ Every person on the leadership team understands their role in building external relationships.
- ☐ All senior leaders, not just those responsible for sales or fundraising, actively build external relationships that benefit the organization.

☐ Board members spend time building relationships on behalf of the organization.

☐ Senior leaders regularly network outside of our local community.

☐ Senior leaders regularly network outside of our industry.

☐ When we need specialized expertise that we don't have in-house, we know who to call.

☐ When looking for new ideas, we have connections outside our industry who will help us.

What was your relationship risk score? If you scored 28 or higher, your organization is a relationship-building star. If you scored 14 or lower, it may be time to rethink your relationship risk.

Are all your senior leaders, including your board, taking on some responsibility for growing the relationship capital of the organization? Is the relationship capital concentrated with one or two individuals? If your organization needed to make connections to powerful leaders in your industry, or in other industries, could you connect to them? Not everyone has to be a super-networker, but if only one or two people are building relationships outside the organization, or worse yet, if no one is, your organization could be at risk.

At best, you are missing out on the benefits of having a rich resource of connections within and outside of your industry. At worst, a single unfortunate event could decimate the relationship capital of your organization. No one person should ever hold all of the relationship capital on behalf of an organization, even a small one. Any organization larger than one person needs to make relationship building a shared responsibility.

ATTRITION

Merriam Webster defines attrition as a reduction in numbers, usually as a result of resignation, retirement, or death. Attrition means that if you are not actively expanding your network of relationships, it is getting ready to retire and move to Florida.

Many years ago, I worked with a foundation here in my hometown. It was a great engagement. We were able to do significant work with the executive director of the foundation and the board. Everyone was happy with the results. After the engagement, I continued to stay in touch with the executive director. He invited me to several industry gatherings with other foundation leaders from across the country, which led to at least one speaking engagement and some great relationship building with other leaders. I was looking forward to continued work with the organization.

Everything was going well . . . until the executive director announced that he was retiring, effective immediately. Now what? What about all the relationship capital I had spent so much time building up with the organization? What would happen to the goodwill, the trust, and the good work that I looked forward to doing in the future?

According to the U.S. Bureau of Labor Statistics in 2020, the average job tenure was 4.1 years. That average tenure has certainly decreased in the aftermath of the COVID-19 pandemic and what many are calling "The Great Resignation."

Unfortunately, that means our networks are constantly changing. People move from one job to another, from one organization to another. People retire. They die. Our business networks are never a static thing. One can never engage people in a business relationship and then assume they will be there forever.

After the first executive director of the foundation retired and moved to Florida, I reached out to the new executive director and shared with her the work we had done, not only for her organization but other work that I thought that she might be interested in. Not only was she very interested in what we had done, she hired us for several additional projects, which have been rewarding for the organization and for us. When she retired recently, she made sure to introduce me to the incoming executive director, and I have also done several projects with her as well.

We can never take for granted that our network will stay the same. If you are not actively growing and expanding your network, then it is shrinking.

For a quick way to see how attrition is impacting your network, do the following exercise.

1. Pick ten people at random from your contact list. If you want to go all out and truly make this a random exercise, visit www.random.org for some easy-to-use and helpful randomization tools.

2. Look up each of the ten people on LinkedIn.

3. How many of the ten people have changed positions or companies in the last year? How many have retired?

4. Add up the number of people who have changed roles or retired and project that percentage onto your entire contact list. How many total people is that?

5. Compare that number to the total number of people you have added to your contact list in the last year.

If you are not actively expanding your network, then it is shrinking. Granted, just because someone has taken on a new role or changed companies does not necessarily mean that they have left your network. But those are often the times when we fall out of touch with each other. And retirement definitely equals a change in roles.

It takes intentional work to grow relationships faster than our network shrinks.

INNOVATION

In his book on innovation and entrepreneurship, Peter Drucker outlined seven sources of innovation.[3] Only one of those sources of innovation comes from inside of an organization: unexpected successes or failures. The other six sources of innovation require information that comes from outside of an organization. These are:

- ☐ Incongruities
- ☐ Process deficiencies taken for granted
- ☐ Industry or market changes that surprise
- ☐ Demographic changes
- ☐ Changes in perception
- ☐ New knowledge

While it is possible to employ an expert team of market researchers to keep tabs on all these sources of innovation, the wise leader will also want to hear about changes in the marketplace firsthand, and the best way to do that is through personal conversations with other leaders and experts that one trusts.

In a 1999 article in the *Harvard Business Review*, it outlined 3M's innovation practices, which included convening teams of experts from other industries and engaging them in brainstorming sessions designed to solve specific innovation challenges. And even though the article is now more than twenty years old, the principal still applies: accessing expertise outside of one's company or industry can lead to creative breakthroughs for organizations.[4]

It may be easy for a company like 3M to dial up and pay handsomely for a team of experts to help with innovation challenges, but most small business or nonprofit leaders don't have the kind of financial resources to accomplish that. However, we do have the potential for building the kind of relationship capital that will enable us to identify thought leaders and other experts who would be willing to help us out if we asked.

Everyone needs at least three of each of the following types of relationships in their network. To qualify, this is someone who would answer your email or phone call (extra points if you can text them).

1. A subject matter expert in your own industry.
2. A thought leader or subject matter expert in an industry that is similar to yours, or often intersects with yours.
3. A thought leader in an industry that is outside of your industry.

What's the difference between a subject matter expert and a thought leader? A subject matter expert is someone who possesses a high level of knowledge about a specific subject or technical expertise. They don't need to be well-known; they only need to be good at what they do. They can be very helpful in solving specific problems. A thought leader (or influencer) is someone whose opinion is highly regarded (think junior high popular kid) and who is widely known.

If you don't have a list of relationships outside of your industry with people you would trust to work on your business challenges, your network isn't big enough.

NETWORKING WHEN YOU
DON'T NEED TO

Relationship giants network all of the time, not just when they need something. Most of the individuals I spoke with have achieved significant career success, so most of them are in high demand from others who want to network with them. Even so, networking continues to be part of their professional lives, even if they don't necessarily need to network to advance their careers. It is just part of who they are.

They advise others to network before they need to—before they are looking for a job, before drumming up new business, or before new opportunities—and to approach networking as an opportunity rather than a necessary evil. Mike Salokas, human resource strategist, says, "It's your responsibility to develop relationships within your profession while you are gainfully employed. Network when you are not looking for a job."[5]

According to one of my business interviews, when it's something that you think of as less than savory, you won't do it. These individuals tend to view networking as something welcome, as simply making new friends, as an extension of how they conduct their professional and personal lives. Another interviewee shared that he is always looking over the landscape for connections, for himself and for others. This generosity of connections always blesses him.

This book will lay out a game plan for creating the kind of business relationships that help you increase trust, reduce risk, counter attrition, and leverage innovation, even if you aren't one of those people who is a natural networker. Anyone can get better at relationships.

And if you are the leader of a team, this book will guide you through a process of helping your team build the relationships that your business needs to grow. It will show you how even the most inward-focused team members can contribute their gifts to building strong relationships.

KEY TAKEAWAYS

- Business is a poor imitation of junior high, and it's still important to know the right people to get things done effectively.
- Every leader needs an intentional relationship-building strategy to 1) build trust, 2) mitigate business risk, 3) counter relationship attrition, and 4) spark innovation.
- Everyone, no matter who they are, can be better at building meaningful business relationships.

CHAPTER 4

WHAT MAKES A GREAT TEAM RELATIONSHIP CODE?

A Relationship Code is the approach that you, your team, and your organization take to build strong, mutually beneficial business relationships. It is a guide that lets you think less about the *how* of building relationships and be fully present for the people you want to connect with. It is based on your values and the values of your organization. It encourages everyone to participate in building relationships using their strengths and ensures that no one person is responsible for all the relationships of the organization. It helps you hold people accountable. More importantly, it helps you make sure that you and everyone in your organization is treating people in a way that matches your organization's values.

A good Relationship Code satisfies three requirements.

1. *Intentional.* Just like your strategic plan, your marketing and sales plan, and your operations plan, your Relationship Code gives you a plan that you and your team can follow. It sets

measurable objectives, and it gives you a way to know how you are doing against that plan. It does not leave networking to chance or to the initiative of one or two super-networkers. Everyone knows what their responsibilities are, and progress toward a shared relationship goal can be measured.

2. *Generous.* A great Relationship Code recognizes the importance of putting the other person at the center of the relationship. Networking is not about seeing how much you can get from someone. A good Relationship Code recognizes that the best relationships are mutually beneficial, that both parties give and take. A good Relationship Code acts as a reminder of this and holds people accountable for making sure that everyone is mindful of what the other person or organization in the relationship brings to the relationship and how they will benefit.

3. *Collaborative.* Everyone runs up against the limitations of Dunbar's Number—the maximum number of meaningful relationships we can sustain at one time—at some point. Everyone has the same amount of time in a day, and no single person can accomplish all of the relationship requirements for growing a business. There is an end to every person's ability to grow their relationship network. A good Relationship Code is collaborative in that it recognizes the relationship strengths of everyone in the organization, including board members, senior leaders, and others. When everyone is working together to create great business relationships, everyone benefits.

WHAT A RELATIONSHIP CODE IS NOT

A Relationship Code should not be confused with a sales or marketing plan, a social media strategy, or any other kind of one-to-many communications' strategy. A Relationship Code is specifically designed to be a plan for how an organizational leader, or a group of leaders, are going to build their business networks on behalf of the organization. A good Relationship Code will support sales, marketing, social media, communications, and all other one-to-many strategies for the organization.

Back to Dunbar's Number. Any person is only capable of maintaining about 150 individual relationships. Therefore everyone who starts out with a Relationship Code and works it successfully will also need to supplement their individual relationship-building strategies with appropriate marketing, social media, and other one-to-many communication techniques. This is a natural progression of good relationship building. One-to-one relationship building and one-to-many relationship building work hand in hand. They support and complement each other, and it is impossible to do one well without doing the other well.

These strategies work in reverse as well. When an organization is doing a good job in its marketing and communications efforts, it is attracting a growing number of individuals who are interested in its content, its mission, and what it has to say about the world. Hidden in this growing number of customers/constituents are individuals who the organization should be cultivating in its individual business networks and should be getting to know better because they represent the kinds of individuals that the senior leaders would benefit from knowing and networking with. A good Relationship Code will include a plan to identify and reach out to these individuals as part of the networking strategy.

THE INTENTIONAL RELATIONSHIP CODE

A good Relationship Code is intentional. It gently takes even the most reluctant networker by the hand and gives them a guide, a road map to success. Because it provides a step-by-step process and is laid out in a logical format, it becomes something that anyone can implement, even those who are not comfortable with the networking process.

At its core, a good Relationship Code identifies the goals of the relationship-building efforts so that everyone understands why we are doing this and what we hope to accomplish through it. This keeps everyone on the same page. We all do better when we understand the *why* of what we are doing.

An intentional Relationship Code will include the following components.

- *A specific goal of relationship-building that is measurable.* It is important that everyone understands this goal and that there is buy-in from everyone who is part of the relationship-building process.

- *A defined set of activities that each person will be responsible for, and a way to measure if they are completing the activities.* This is a way to hold people accountable for activities. In networking, just like in sales, it is important to remember that the activities involve two parties. We are responsible for our actions, but we can't be held responsible for the reactions of others. Therefore, when we define the activities that we are going to engage in, we don't necessarily measure the other person's response; we measure the activities. For example, I can say that I am going to meet with ten people in a week with the goal of identifying one next step in each meeting. I can hold myself accountable to that set of activities because those things are in my control. I can't hold myself accountable for what the other person will do in those meetings because that is beyond my control. If, in each one of those meetings, the other party decides they do not want to meet with me again, it's likely that I didn't do a good job of presenting myself and my case for a continued relationship. But it's still their decision not to meet again, and I can't control their decisions. The Relationship Code outlines activities that I can control and be held accountable for. It does not stipulate what others will do as a result of my activities.

- *A defined set of individuals who are preferred targets of relationship building with a specific rationale that aligns with the overall goal of the relationship-building efforts.* For example, at Outsight Network, the primary goal of relationship building is to grow the business. Therefore our primary target of relationship building are individuals who have the capacity to engage our consulting services. In our case, these are typically CEOs, board members, or chief marketing and chief development officers of organizations that are driven by mission and values.

THE GENEROUS RELATIONSHIP CODE

A good Relationship Code is generous. It ensures that everything we do in building relationships is done not just for our benefit but also for the benefit of those we are in relationship with. Networking is never a one-way process. It is never solely about getting something from the person, or coercing them to do something for us, or tricking them into doing us a favor. It especially is not about doing something for them so that they will be obligated to do something for us in return. In fact, the first step in building a relationship is *not* doing someone a favor. It is asking them to say yes to something small and easy for them to say yes to.

A generous Relationship Code creates guidelines to help us understand what the other person wants and needs and lays the foundation for a relationship that makes sure that both parties benefit. One-sided relationships always end up being short-term, and short-term relationships are not the goal. The goal of a Relationship Code is to form lasting relationships that benefit everyone.

A generous Relationship Code will include the following components:

- *A clear definition of what we bring to the relationship and what the other person brings to the relationship.* The goal of relationship building is balance. Great relationships are never one-sided. If we are the only ones to bring value, we end up being taken advantage of. If we only care about what the other person can do for us, we come off as manipulative, and people will quickly tire of us.

- *An understanding of what we are willing to give up to make the relationship work.* I have had the privilege in my career of facilitating a number of successful collaborative initiatives between organizations. The best, most successful and long-term collaborations, just like relationships, happen because each organization involved is willing to give up something to work together. The benefit of what can be done together outweighs whatever it is the organization must give up. In some cases, the organizations give up financial resources to make a collaboration work. In other cases, they give up the time of a senior leader to spearhead the initiative. In still others, they must make the choice to abandon other initiatives to make the collaboration work. As we network with others, we will need to make the same kinds of choices.

- *A goal for what we will receive from each relationship, even if it is only to learn more about the other person or discover what they might be able to bring to the table.* It is not selfish to want to receive something from our business relationships. It is why we engage in networking. However, the objective should never be the sole focus, divorced from what we bring and what we are willing to give up.

NETWORKING FOR THE BENEFIT OF OTHERS

Most of the relationship giants I spoke with are in professional positions where many people are seeking to connect with them. They seemingly have no need to build their networks any further, and yet they continue to make time for networking? Why is that?

They continue to network because, for them, networking is about how they can be of benefit to someone else, not what is in it for them. This is what sets these relationship giants apart. Networking is not a transaction or a way to get something from someone else. It is about building long-term relationships with the goal of learning about the other person and exploring ways that they can be of service to them.

One individual described it as a dance in which they are adding value to others. Over time, that value comes back to them in many ways. Another asks himself if he can serve the people he is meeting disproportionately well. In other words, is he meeting people for whom he can be an asset?

A common characteristic of those I spoke to is a genuine curiosity about others without needing anything in return. In most discussions, I experienced this for myself as those I interviewed also wanted to learn about me and my work. These individuals trust that good things will come from showing a genuine interest in serving others without expectation. Greater opportunities will always come from genuine service, and they trust in that outcome. But it is never the primary reason why they engage in relationships.

THE COLLABORATIVE RELATIONSHIP CODE

Business networking is a team sport. If you are a senior leader in a for-profit or nonprofit organization, relationship building is your primary role, but it is also the responsibility of your board members and your senior team. Even if you are the sole proprietor of a business, you are never alone in building business relationships. There are often associations, networking groups, and even family members who are willing to partner with you to build business relationships on behalf of your business.

Every one of us quickly runs into our limitations of time, resources, energy, capacity, and everything else that makes us human. We cannot singlehandedly grow all of the network relationships we need. This is especially true for organizations that must raise money to support their work, or that are in growth mode, or whose industry is rapidly changing. Pretty much every organization in today's economy requires a team relationship-building effort to be successful.

A collaborative Relationship Code will include the following components, which I will walk you through in more detail in chapters 6 through 14:

- *A list of everyone who contributes to the relationship capital of the organization.* Again, even a sole proprietor of a business will have family members, associates, friends, and other people who are ready, willing, and able to make referrals and act as a support network to you as you grow your business.
- *A list of the relationship-building style and strengths of each member of the team.* This comprehensive view of all of your network assets allows you to assign responsibilities and goals to each member of the team based on their own comfort level. Remember, we are starting in our comfort zone and pushing the edges of it. Everyone is different;

therefore everyone has a different style. People will more quickly find success if they start with where they are and practice growing from there.

- *A defined set of activities and goals for each member of the team.* Because each person is different, each person on the team will have a different set of goals and activities, ones that they can accomplish and contribute to the overall relationship-building goal of the organization.

EVERYONE'S NETWORK IS DIFFERENT

In one of my client engagements, I was asked to work with the executive director and board chair of a nonprofit organization. The organization was growing rapidly and had just launched a successful program in its city and was searching for its next initiative. As I met with the two leaders and did an assessment of the organization, its leadership, its brand, and its vision for the community, it became apparent that both of these leaders were natural networkers. They had created a successful organization because they are both very good at building relationships and had leveraged that ability on behalf of the organization.

However, each of their networks was very different. They traveled in different circles and had come to the organization with a completely different set of relationships. There was very little overlap in their networks when they joined the organization. They were able to create a successful organization because they each focused on building a network that would support the organization from their position of strength. In fact, the organization has become known for its ability to work across multiple networks because these two individuals intentionally collaborated in their networking efforts, each reaching into their networks and bringing a diverse group of relationships to the organization.

In addition to being intentional, generous, and collaborative, a good Relationship Code will spell out specific elements, including the who, what, where, when, and why of relationship building for both individuals and for teams. Each situation is unique, and the answers will be different for every person and every team. Because people have different goals for their Relationship Code, there is no single right answer for any of these elements. Instead, each individual and each team must define these based on what they want to accomplish with their Relationship Code.

WHO

This is the delineation of who you will meet with. This can be defined as narrowly or as broadly as you would like. It may be defined differently based on who is doing the networking. For example, a CEO of an organization will want to network with CEOs of supplier organizations and other key partners, as well as customers. They will network with potential board members and will also want to network with leaders in other industries.

Leaders who are nearing a transition will want to network more broadly so that they cross paths with potential successors.

Board members of nonprofit organizations will want to focus on networking with key donors and other potential supporters. They will want to build relationships with leaders of other nonprofits that may be potential collaboration partners. They will also want to maintain relationships with recipients of the service to help them understand their perspective and how the organization impacts the lives of these important constituents.

Leaders responsible for sales and marketing will, of course, focus primarily on current and prospective customers. At the same time, they will want to make some room to network with salespeople in other companies and industries to stay abreast of market changes. It is particularly helpful to understand what is happening in industries that are tangential to one's own. For example, because so many of my clients are nonprofit organizations, I often network with leaders in the financial industry because market performance trends have a significant impact on donations to nonprofit organizations.

As the organization grows and its needs change, it will be important to revisit the definition of *who*. There may be shifting priorities in who the leaders need to connect to. For example, those who are dealing with new challenges will want to reach outside of their industry for business models and solutions that may be applicable to the challenge but have not yet been implemented in your industry.

In answering the who question, most organizations will want to make room for networking beyond the usual suspects. If your competitors are networking only in limited silos, only in your industry, and only with the well-known thought leaders, you will gain a significant edge by networking more broadly and creating access to market intelligence beyond what your competitors have access to. It gives you a broader viewpoint and makes you more valuable to your clients and your organization as someone who sees the big picture.

WHAT

The Relationship Code will provide a guideline for what you will do with each person in your network. The goal will be to keep moving the relationship toward mutual benefit so that each person in the business relationship benefits. The *what* is a road map to get there. This can be as prescriptive as outlining a set of steps to move through for each person. For those who are not as comfortable with networking, this prescriptive approach is often helpful.

On the other hand, those who are already comfortable with networking and do it easily will probably not want detailed steps that guide them through a relationship. In this case, the *what* will more likely be a set of general guidelines that serve as reminders of the types of activities that move relationships toward the goal and offer much greater latitude for the individual to go with their instincts on the most logical next step.

Personally, I find that I spend way too much time staring at contacts in my database, wondering what to do next with them. In my case, I appreciate a checklist of possibilities, all of which I know will help move the relationship forward. I need a list of suggestions to help make the process of networking more efficient for me.

Even more helpful is to define the *what* immediately after each connection. For example, my goal is to walk out of every meeting with a specific set of next steps defined, even if I don't implement them until much later. If I walk out of a meeting and the next step is to reconnect with someone in six months' time, I make sure that I also note exactly how I am going to reach out to the person and the topic of conversation. I often find it is helpful to frame this as a question that I want to ask next to keep the conversation going.

Knowing your *what* is much like the process of planning a meal. Having someone plan your menus and do your grocery shopping for you makes the whole process much faster and requires less mental energy. Because you are always prepared and you have the right materials on hand, the planning part is taken care of for you, the preparation becomes easy, and you spend less time aimlessly standing in front of your refrigerator.

The goal of the *what* in the Relationship Code is to keep you from spending time standing in front of your database, staring at your contacts, and wondering what to do next. It makes you significantly more effective in your networking time, and the results, like your dinner, will be much tastier.

WHERE

Answering the *where* of networking and how it is applied is a deeply personal, and deeply important part of business networking. *Where* defines how you will reach out to people. In this age of social media and multiple communication channels, I believe *where* is one of the most important decisions you can make regarding networking. It is deeply personal because everyone has different styles of communication and different communication habits. This is particularly true now that we have five generations of workers in the workforce.

When I first started my career, the telephone was the primary mode of communication. Fax machines were relatively new, and I still remember the days when I was in charge of managing the office courier service. Yes, we actually paid someone to hand deliver communications across town. Then the fax machine came into wider practice, and we no longer sent things by "action messenger." Because my husband ran his business out of our home, we were one of the first ones to have a fax machine. At the time, our young son couldn't understand why he couldn't fax one of his drawings to his friend who lived in a different neighborhood. I had to explain to him that his friend didn't have any way of receiving the fax.

When we called someone in those days, if they weren't at their desk, we got a helpful receptionist or admin who took our message on a pink notepad (extra points to anyone who still has one of those notepads on their desk). That was also a time when most people returned a call. We didn't have phones to take with us, and we were diligent to return all those calls listed on those pink memo pads.

There are still relics among us, like me, who prefer picking up the phone and having a direct conversation, even if I have to schedule it in advance. I also prefer meeting someone face-to-face. There is something about being in the same room, being able to read their body language, being able to shake hands in greeting and to say goodbye that can never be replaced by video conference, no matter how good the technology gets.

But I have learned some people under the age of thirty-five prefer text as a means of communication. I even have a sixty-something colleague who announced that he would no longer respond to email but would only use text messaging from that point forward. I try to pay attention to his wishes. And that's the point. *Where* is not about my preferences and the way I like to connect. It is about paying attention to what methods the other person prefers and reaching out to them in the way they most appreciate it.

Because we have so many choices and so many options, and because we are all so different in our experiences, paying attention to the preferred *where* of our relationships is the right thing to do. I take my cues from how others reach out to me. LinkedIn messages? I always respond on LinkedIn. Did they reach out to me last via email? I make sure I reply that way. And if I'm not sure, I try different methods until I get a response. If they don't answer a phone call, I try email next. If that doesn't work, I try a social media channel—without pestering people and being obnoxious.

WHEN

There is a rhythm to building a business network, and there is an appropriate frequency to how often to connect with people in our network. Much of this depends on the individual, who they are, and how we are connected to them.

Relationships are never static. They are either speeding up or slowing down. This is what I refer to as *relationship velocity*. Velocity is determined by what kind of person we are networking with, how much of a priority we are to each other, and what we are doing together. A person might be a very high priority, but we don't have a close connection to them. That means their velocity is slower than someone with whom we are working closely on a project. Velocity determines how frequently we connect to someone. This also prevents spending a lot of time staring at our database, wondering what to do next.

Knowing the *when* of networking provides a guideline that keeps us from being creepy, and also keeps us from losing touch with people who are important to us. When we segment our contacts by type and then create a frequency of connection, depending on that type, it takes so much of the effort out of networking and keeps us in front of the people who are most important to us. It also helps us prioritize the time we spend networking.

We balance frequency with the needs of the person we are connecting to. We take our cue from them. If they speed up the relationship by reaching out to us more frequently, we can decide that we will match their speed. We can also decide not to respond to their cues and slow the relationship down. The point is that we need to decide on *when* with intentionality and not let circumstances decide it for us. This changing velocity also helps to bring balance to our portfolio of relationships, allowing you us focus on faster relationships even while others are slowing down.

WHY

Why can be the most challenging aspect of a relationship. I have found that the best relationships are those in which both people understand the *why* of it. In the book *The Collaboration Challenge*, James Austin writes about effective cross-sector partnerships. Through researching successful case studies, he identifies the seven components that make these partnerships work. One of these is *clarity of purpose*. Austin states that all parties in a collaborative project need to articulate what they expect to accomplish, and that it is perfectly acceptable, even imperative, for all parties to receive value from the collaboration.[1]

The same is true for networking relationships. It is far easier to establish a relationship if both parties understand why they are there and how they can benefit from the relationship. It means both people must come to the table with something to offer and some idea of what they can accomplish together that they can't do on their own. It's okay if this is not apparent at first. That is part of the discovery process of a relationship. That may take some time. But if the *why* does not emerge over the course of at least a couple of conversations, the relationship will probably fade away.

Because Outsight Network's business model relies on partnerships with other subject matter experts, part of our role is to identify talent that would be of help to our clients, so we often meet with individuals who are consultants or are considering becoming consultants. Sometimes we share similar target audiences, values, and our approach to consulting. However, if there is nothing for us to do together, it becomes more difficult to maintain a relationship. If the only *why* of these relationships is to find new business, they will always be one-dimensional and transactional. The best why's are multidimensional; they give us multiple reasons to continue to connect and bring value to each other.

Now that you have a good understanding of the components of a Relationship Code, you are ready to create your own.

KEY TAKEAWAYS

- A good Relationship Code is intentional. It is approached with a plan and a purpose.
- A good Relationship Code is generous. It serves the needs of everyone involved in the relationship.
- A good Relationship Code is collaborative. It recognizes and affirms the relationship strengths of everyone on the leadership team.
- A good Relationship Code answers: Who? What? Where? When? Why? The answers to these questions make networking easier and more effective.

CHAPTER 5

THE RELATIONSHIP CODE EQUATION

I often wonder how much time I have spent over the years staring at a list of contacts in my CRM and wondering who to reach out to next. It reminds me of the many, many nights I have come home from work and stood at the open door of my refrigerator, wondering what to fix for dinner. By the time I finish a long day at work, I am famished, and my decision-making power is at its weakest. It's why meal-planning apps are so popular, I suppose.

A relationship rating works the same way as a meal-planning app. It makes decision-making easier. In this chapter I will share the relationship equation that has become the foundation for my Relationship Code, and how I arrived at it. While recognizing that everyone is equal in the eyes of God, my Relationship Code also recognizes the reality that my goal as a business leader is to bring value to the people who are most likely to benefit from our services. Not everyone wants or needs what we do, and that's okay.

Many people have told me they are uncomfortable with "rating" everyone they meet, and that it feels disingenuous to true relationship building. But unlimited networking eventually leads to becoming overwhelmed and ineffective. Having some kind of score to assign to people gives you a way to ensure that you are filling your calendar with the right people. It prevents you from engaging in a frantic networking style that overcommits without reaching the outcomes that you need from your networking activity.

Social media has exacerbated the feelings of FOMO—fear of missing out—for many of us. How much of our networking activity is driven by this fear of missing out? Have you ever found your calendar so overbooked that you have declared (even temporarily) that you will no longer do networking meetings? Rating each relationship means that you can also preserve time on your calendar to meet with those who you may not know very well, with those who may not be able to do anything for you, and with those mysterious people who come out of nowhere and turn out to be valuable connections. That's a much better way to love others as ourselves, to make time for those who can't return our favors, as well as making time for those who fit our target audience.

Having a rating to assign to people quickly and easily replaces subjective "in the moment" judgment with an intentional strategy that allows you to prioritize and steward your relationship-building time more effectively. It also prevents you from overlooking those who don't immediately fit your perceived idea of value. It brings discipline to the process so that you have ways of measuring your activities against your goals and making wise adjustments if you aren't yet reaching your goals.

For those who are reluctant networkers, having a relationship rating reminds you that networking is important. It also reminds you why each person is important and nudges you to stay out there and keep working your network, even when you don't feel like it. Doing so is a way to love others as we love ourselves.

The key value of a Relationship Code is that it allows you to make decisions quickly, easily, and consistently. You can do a better job of treating everyone well because you are not making snap judgments about people. You are applying a consistent principle to everyone and allowing the system to drive your decision-making.

In his book *Willpower*, Roy Baumeister makes the case that decision-making taxes our stores of energy and will, and that every decision we make during the day saps some of that energy. He cites his experiments that demonstrates that shoppers in a mall who had already made the most decisions in the stores gave up more quickly when asked to solve simple math problems than the shoppers who had not made as many decisions.[1] The more decisions we make the less willpower we have. Decision-making is a finite resource. It is why we stand at the refrigerator at the end of the day and wonder what we should make for dinner. It is why that decision, at that particular point in the day, is so hard. It is also why we cheat on our diets at the end of the day and then flop down on the couch and binge watch that show we know we really shouldn't waste time on.

Having a Relationship Code that is easy to apply—without judgment, without overthinking, and without too much "in the moment" decision-making—preserves our energy and brain power for other things. It gives the super-networker peace of mind because they can let the system work for them without fearing that they are missing something or someone of value. It gives the reluctant networker encouragement because it means they can be confident that they are doing what they need to do to expand their network and reach their relationship goals.

The Relationship Code equation combines three elements of networking and adds them up to arrive at a single score that can be applied to each individual in your network.

Connection + Alignment + Velocity = Relationship Code Score

Each component of this formula is tailored to the individual and the team that is using it to define their networking relationships. Each

Relationship Code equation will be unique to you and your organization. It is designed to help you reach your relationship-building goals more effectively so that you are stewarding your time wisely and adding value to your organization and to those you are in relationship with.

Ultimately, a relationship score is never a hard-and-fast rule. The goal is to provide a guideline for how to prioritize relationships, which will make that decision-making process easier and more automatic.

CONNECTION

Connection is how we are known by another person. Because relationships take two individuals to be complete, your job is to understand both sides of the relationship: yours and theirs. Your job is to pay attention to the other person as much as you pay attention to yourself. Therefore, when you think about connection, you are thinking about it from the other person's perspective. How do they know you? The goal of this is to identify all the ways that you are known and, especially, all the ways that you want to be known to others. This is your personal brand.

Many years ago, when I had just launched my consulting firm, I was home visiting family for the holidays. At dinner, my adult niece looked at me and said, "Aunt Kay, I love your new website. It's really pretty. But I have no idea what you do." Ouch! While she didn't necessarily represent my target audience, that reminded me that it's not about what I say about myself, or who I think I am; it's about how others know me. I quickly went back to my web site and made some changes.

Also, we can expect there to be a progression to connection. When you start out, the other person does not know you at all. You may have identified them as someone with whom you would like to have a relationship. They might work for an organization you are targeting as a client. It might be an individual whom you admire and would like to learn from. It could be a potential new hire or a potential board member.

The first stage in any relationship starts from the unknown. In other words, the person you are thinking about has no idea who you are.

From there, the relationship progresses through various stages to the place where you are known the way you want to be known by that person. How many stages it progresses through is completely up to you and the way that you build relationships. In the application section of the book, I will guide you through a series of steps that I have used to identify the connection steps for me and my team.

It's important to remember that there are no right or wrong answers when it comes to connection stages. Every person and every organization is different because we all have different relationship styles and different relationship goals. You may have as few as two stages— known and unknown. Or you might have as many as ten. The important thing is that it works for you and is simple enough that you and your team are using it consistently.

I have learned that it is important to identify relationship stages, or how you are known to others in your network, because a significant body of research has shown that as human beings, we progress through stages in all of our personal relationships, not just our business relationships.

A quick Google search on "relationship stages" will yield numerous articles about stages of relationship with our family, friends, and other personal connections. Similarly, our business relationships evolve through stages as well. Andy Lopata's book, *Connected Leadership*, suggests that business relationships can move through up to seven levels of connectedness, beginning with mutual recognition (the people you recognize when you bump into them). At the opposite end of the spectrum are relationships that have moved beyond business and become personal friendships.[2] Not all business relationships progress through all of these stages. It is helpful to overlay this perspective onto our own thinking about how we are typically known by those in our network, and how we would like to be known. It is also helpful to look at your typical sales cycle, if you have defined one for your organization, and think about how this could be aligned with individual networking relationships.

For me, understanding and thinking about how I am known by the other person helps me understand where the relationship is headed next. It makes decisions—such as how frequently to communicate, what to communicate, and how I can best serve the other person—so much easier. I am able to keep notes about this in my CRM system and add contact points to my calendar for future dates. It also means that I am never looking at a calendar appointment six months from now and wondering what I am supposed to say to the person I am about to call. I always have the path in front of me.

But doesn't that process take the joy out of networking? Doesn't that reduce people to automatons? Doesn't it depersonalize us as human beings and let cold, impersonal rules drive our relationships? I hear all of those objections. I particularly hear those objections from people who are naturally good at relationship building and don't necessarily want to have rules imposed on something that they do so easily. I would simply say that these are guidelines that give us more freedom to be present in relationships and free up our brains to focus on the person rather than on how the relationship should go.

Research published in the *Journal of Management* in 2019 suggests that a moderate level of constraints increases creativity and innovation: "Having too few input constraints breeds complacency. A moderate level of input constraints, however, frames the task as a greater challenge and, in turn, motivates experimentation and risk-taking. This moderate level also prompts a mind-set to maximize the creative value generated from available resources, to search for novel combinations using what is at hand, and to think beyond traditional solutions."[3] In other words, when we have the proverbial blank sheet of paper in front of us, we struggle to create. We have too much freedom, and that freedom often paralyzes us.

Understanding the ways in which we want to be known prevents us from staring at a blank sheet of relationship paper and wondering what to do with it. It is a framework for the creative expression of our relationship capital. It guides us to act in ways that put the other person at the center of the relationship. It keeps you from always putting yourself and your needs at the center of every meeting, every email, and every connection. It reminds you to proceed toward a goal that is not only good for you but makes sense to, and is good for, the other person.

As an example, the highest connection in Outsight's relationship score equation is an individual who has already worked with us and with multiple members of our network of talented consultants. They have a much richer experience of the fullness of our brand than someone who has worked with just one of us.

ALIGNMENT

The second part of the Relationship Code Equation is alignment. Alignment is the level to which the other person is aligned with you, with your goals, and with the values of your organization. This is probably the most difficult and subjective of all the ways to view your relationships. It involves a judgment call, or a series of judgment calls.

At the same time, it is probably the most important aspect of how you measure relationships because it lies at the core of whether you want to be in relationship with someone or not. If you are working toward the same goals and you share the same values, you intrinsically know that the relationship will benefit both of you, and it makes sense that if you work together, you will both benefit.

For the reluctant networker, it is helpful to see how closely someone aligns with your goals and values. It offers a sense of assurance that you are connecting with people who share your values and are working toward the same ends that you are. It can help motivate you to go out and make connections, even if it is not your strong suit. It helps get you out the door.

For the super-networker, a strong alignment score acts more like a guardrail on relationship building. It helps to prioritize precious networking time and places the focus on those individuals who are most closely aligned with what you are trying to accomplish. Again, it is not meant to be arbitrary or onerous. It is meant to be a shorthand to help you prioritize and steward your relationship-building time. It may feel mercenary in the beginning. However, it is important to remember that the goal of this exercise is to make more effective use of your time and your relationship-building efforts.

Alignment is not meant to be a tool to keep people out of your circle based on their belief systems, or any other "category" that so easily divides us. The goal of networking is not to be exclusive. It is meant to protect your time so that you can choose to be inclusive in your relationship-building efforts. It's not that you only want to connect to people who are just like you. That would defeat one of the primary reasons for expanding your network: to expose yourself and your organization to new ideas and new relationships. It does mean that you can intentionally focus your time proportionally, making room for those new ideas and new relationships while paying appropriate attention to all of your relationships.

There are multiple types and multiple levels of alignment. The ways that we can measure alignment within our network are almost limitless. Alignment measurement should take into account your corporate and individual values. It should take into account your corporate goals and any new initiatives that you are pursuing. It should also be easy to estimate and easy for everyone to understand. It will mostly be subjective, and that is okay. Speed is important, and this is one of those areas where "gut instinct" is perfectly acceptable.

Early in my career, I was pitching a strategic planning and research project to the board of a faith-based organization. When it came time for questions from the board members, one person spoke up from the back of the room saying, "Who are you to tell us what to do? I mean, are you even (insert denomination name here)?" Clearly, this person was using shared theological beliefs as a measure of alignment and had decided that only if I was part of his "system" would he consider me to be in alignment. I, on the other hand, immediately knew that this person probably didn't share my value of considering outside perspectives and different points of view, so my estimation of our alignment went down.

If there are multiple people in your organization who are taking on relationship-building responsibilities, everyone should have a shared understanding of what alignment looks like in practice. How do you know if your team is assessing alignment consistently? One of the best ways is to define your relationship equation as a team and then work through multiple relationships to see if everyone would apply the equation to every contact in the same way. If there are disagreements, then it is time to go back to the relationship equation and work through it until everyone can apply it consistently. In the next section of the book we will share a set of tools to help teams define alignment so that they can apply it consistently to all relationships.

It is also important to have a "benefit of the doubt" category when it comes to alignment. Sometimes we need to give people the benefit of the doubt and not make an assessment too quickly or one based on too little knowledge. It is too important to miss out on relationship potential just because you didn't know enough about someone initially.

Just like connection, alignment can be as simple as a yes or no, or it could be a scale. I would suggest no more than a five-point scale. The goal is to create something that people will use and will speed up relationship building rather than get in the way of it.

LOOK FOR VALUES ALIGNMENT

I asked each of the relationship giants I spoke with if there is ever a time when they say no when it comes to relationship building. Most of them agree that what we often think of as networking is a waste of time and does nothing to build true, authentic relationship. One described it as an implicit belief that networking is about using people. That it is a self-centered act. And if one holds this belief, it will make genuine relationship building much more difficult to do.

These relationship giants are constantly on the lookout for relationships with people who share their value of putting others first. Some named specific clues they look for in another person. For example, if someone they meet does most of the talking the first meeting, they are unlikely to meet with them again. Another described people who are know-it-alls without being experts as someone they will say no to. Most say that self-interest is easy to spot in others.

Most importantly, they will say no to a networking request if they believe they can't add value to the other person. Several said that they will refer people to someone else if they can't be of help. Others said that they are careful to be very clear in their communications and not create expectations that they can't meet. "Clear is kind," in the words of one interviewee.

VELOCITY

Velocity is the measure of the speed of a relationship. Relationships are never a static thing. They are either speeding up or they are slowing down. This is part of the natural, healthy life cycle of relationships. Not all relationships are increasingly moving toward a mutual goal. Sometimes they are slowing down. That is not a bad thing. Relationships, particularly business relationships, naturally go through ebbs and flows. Sometimes we are working very intensely together toward a common goal. In this case, the relationship could be described as speeding up. Other times, we have finished a specific initiative or task with a network partner, and we both need to go and implement the idea in our own organization or community. In that case, the relationship is slowing down, which is part of the natural course.

Sometimes relationships hit a wall. We can only progress so far before some barrier, either on our side or on the side of the other, prevents us from progressing. Here, too, we think of the relationship as having slowed down. Based on my experience of thirty years building a business network, in most cases, I can walk away from a phone call or a meeting and decide quickly if the relationship is speeding up or slowing down. Speeding up means there was something that happened that indicated both parties want to continue talking, and there is some mutual goal or idea that they want to continue working on together. In most cases, there is a specific next step that has been named and agreed upon. There is also a specific timeline for getting it done, and someone has taken on the responsibility for the next step. Quite often there is an agreement to come back together at a specific time or date. This is an example of a relationship that is speeding up.

If any of those are missing, chances are the relationship is slowing down. In my experience, the greatest barrier to velocity in relationships is that people have not figured out what they can do together. They may like each other immensely. They may be completely aligned in goals and values. But if they can't figure out what the next step is, the relationship has slowed down significantly and is in danger of stopping completely.

I often experience this in meeting other consultants. Because our business model is a network of consultants, many people come to Outsight Network hoping to work with our clients. I love these kinds of connections and always welcome the opportunity to meet someone who shares my love of consulting and is committed to doing great work for great leaders and their organizations. Too often, however, each of us come into the meeting with different expectations. Initially I am there because I want to learn about a new potential resource for my clients, and to hear what another consultant is observing in the marketplace. I am always on the lookout for new ideas and new talent.

Too often, the other person is expecting that I will have an immediate opening for them on a current project. I get it. It's tough out there, and most independent consultants, and even those in firms, are constantly searching for new business. Most of us pursue this profession because there is something that we do incredibly well, and we love to do it. We love to bless our clients and see them succeed. But most of us don't love to sell ourselves. We find it a little awkward and sometimes embarrassing to say we need more work. Wouldn't it be wonderful if there was a way to do what we do without having to sell what we do?

The result is that the relationship often doesn't progress past the first meeting. We haven't found anything that we can do together immediately, something that will form the foundation of the relationship. We need to be engaged in some mutual goal or activity, even a tiny one, for the relationship to gain some velocity. Without that, it slows down and decreases in velocity. Until something comes up that we can do together, it will continue to slow down.

As time passes, unless something happens, all relationships tend to slow down. Personally, I find it hard to see client projects come to an end, especially when I have formed a great working relationship with them.

Honestly, at the end of a project, I often feel like I'm standing outside my client's door with my nose pressed to the glass saying, "Remember me? Remember how much fun we had?" I once even volunteered my time and paid my own way to a two-day meeting with a client's Madison Avenue advertising agency after my official role in the project was finished just so I could avoid that feeling. Fortunately, I have since found less-expensive ways to keep in touch, and I have learned that slowing down is a natural progression of a working relationship.

Like the other elements of the Relationship Code equation, velocity can be as simple as speeding up or slowing down. Or it can be a scale. Whether simple or complex, it should serve the purpose of making networking more efficient for you and your organization.

PUTTING IT ALL TOGETHER

Relationship value—the sum of connection, alignment, and velocity of a relationship—becomes a helpful tool that allows you to steward your network well without wasting time on relationships that do not benefit both your organization and your constituents. I have found that it should never be the only factor I consider in building my business relationships. However, it can be a central tool that helps speed up decision-making and ensures that I am spending time on the most important relationships.

KEY TAKEAWAYS

- Using a metric for relationship management saves time and decision-making effort. It also ensures that you are focusing on the relationships that are most important for your organization and your constituents.
- Connection + Alignment + Velocity = Relationship Value
- We assign these measures based on how the other person in the relationship views you.

- Connection is how you are known to the other person.
- Alignment is based on shared values and goals.
- Velocity is a changing measure of where the relationship is headed—speeding up or slowing down.
- A great relationship value measurement is one that is simple enough that you will use it.

CHAPTER 6

IDENTIFY YOUR KEY RELATIONSHIP TYPES

A re you ready to get started working your own Relationship Code? This section of the book will walk you through the eight easy steps that I have used on my path to my own relationship-building code. This is the compilation of everything I have learned on my thirty-year journey from super-introvert to super-networker. If you are working with a team, you will want to work through these steps for yourself first. Feel free to skip over steps that don't apply to you, or work in a different order. There is no right or wrong way to do this. In chapter 14 I will share what I have learned about creating a team version of a Relationship Code.

Some helpful advice: If you work with a CRM or database system, it's important to do all the planning on paper first before you make any changes to your technology. Do not make any changes to your database until you have completed this section on paper and everyone on your team is fully on board with the decisions, the process, and the way that you will be managing relationships from this point forward. It will be much easier to think it all through first before you start implementing and changing the database structure.

This section is organized into eight specific steps. Many of the steps include tools or templates that have helped me and will help you create your own Relationship Code. You can download all of the template documents at www.kayedwardsauthor.com/templates.

I have found the best way to implement your Relationship Code is to follow the steps in order, from one through eight. Complete the tools for each step so that you have a written record of the decisions you have made. If you can't decide, it's okay to use your best guess and come back later. There are no right or wrong answers, and everyone's Relationship Code will be different. All that matters is that it works for you

STEP ONE: IDENTIFY KEY RELATIONSHIP TYPES

The first step in creating your Relationship Code is deciding what kinds of people you want to focus on. It is important to note that I said, "focus on." One of the benefits of a Relationship Code is that it allows you to prioritize your networking time so that you are "majoring on the majors." You are spending the bulk of your relationship time with individuals who are most important to your organization. At the same time, it helps you preserve some time for serendipitous connections, those people you're not sure about, or may not seem like they fit your target audience but could be diamonds in the rough.

The goal of identifying your Key Relationship types is to be able to budget your relationship-building time so that you are receiving the greatest benefits from your time investment. While it's great to meet with everyone who reaches out to you, and some of us may be in professional positions where this is possible, it's also important to achieve your relationship-building goals, and not everyone who wants to meet with you will help you to do that. Sometimes it will be wise to say no, or to pass a relationship on to someone else on your team. Identifying your relationship priorities will help you do that with integrity.

To identify your Key Relationship types, first list all the types of individuals that are a part of your organization's success. At this point, make the list as comprehensive as possible. You are not listing individual names. Instead, you are listing types of individuals who contribute to the success of your organization, even if in a small way. Some might call these stakeholders. Some call them constituents. It is broader than just customers. For example, at Outsight we serve leaders of organizations. Some of them lead for-profit organizations, some of them lead nonprofit organizations. We also often work with board members of both for-profit and nonprofit organizations. In addition to organizational leaders, we often interact with other employees of an organization. Because they also contribute to our success, we list them as a type of individual with which we interact. Vendors and suppliers also contribute to our success because they provide components of our services to clients.

For some organizations there is an end-user of your product or service who does not necessarily purchase directly from you. For manufacturers, customers may use the product but may purchase through a distributor rather than directly from the manufacturer. Nonprofit organizations often have constituents who are direct recipients of the organization's services—for example, people who are served by the nonprofit but who do not pay for the service.

For nonprofit organizations, it is helpful to understand the specific business model in which your organization operates in order to identify all of the constituents of your organization. According to the Stanford Social Innovation Review, there are ten nonprofit business models, with different combinations of constituents for each. A study of this research can be helpful in identifying your constituents.[1] One common example is a hospital or university where all constituents pay a fee for service. Some also give charitable donations out of gratitude for what that service has done in their lives. Another common example is an organization that grants wishes to terminally ill children where the donors and the recipients of the organization's work tend not to overlap.

Once you have thought about your business model and all the types of individuals who contribute to the success of your business model, sit down with the following chart and list as many individual types as you possibly can. The goal is quantity. Don't worry at this point about prioritizing. Just get as many different types of individuals on the list as possible. You can download the template at www.kayedwardsauthor. com/templates.

KEY RELATIONSHIP TYPES

What kinds of people contribute to the success of your business?

PRIMARY RELATIONSHIP TYPES	SECONDARY RELATIONSHIP TYPES	ADDITIONAL RELATIONSHIP TYPES

Don't forget people who may have an indirect impact on your organization. For example, government officials, neighbors, journalists, bloggers, or other key influencers in your industry who could be included on this list.

The next step is to look at your list and think about any logical groupings in each of the columns. The goal is to make the list shorter so that you can start to prioritize. For example, I could look at my list and easily see that all consultants, whether they work for firms or are independent practitioners, could be grouped into one category. On the other hand, CEOs of consulting firms belong in their own category because they have a different scope of responsibility and a different type of relationship with Outsight. They are in a position, for example, to partner with Outsight in a different way than an independent practitioner is. I can also look at my list and see that all C-level leaders and board members can be grouped into a single category because they all have a level of decision-making power that means they can hire Outsight on behalf of their organizations. The goal is to consolidate all types of individuals into no more than four or five categories. For most people, this is a manageable number of relationship types to keep track of.

Once you have thought through logical groupings and noted them on the chart, it is time to prioritize. Look at all the groups and decide which one contributes most to the success of your organization. For most people, it will be people who directly pay for your product or service. Even if you aren't directly in a sales role, you likely have some responsibility for interacting with those you would consider your customers. For nonprofit leaders, Key Relationship types will likely include major donors, board members, key partners, and the people your organization serves.

Circle up to three groups that represent your Key Relationship types and number them in priority order. These are the types of individuals you will be focusing on, intentionally spending the bulk of your relationship-building time on those who have the potential to create the greatest benefit for your organization.

As you complete your Key Relationships Chart and group them into major categories, it may be that you have more than three categories. This is okay for now. Later, you can identify ways to engage those who fall below your top-three priorities. For now, you have successfully identified your Key Relationships. Congratulations.

CHAPTER 7

PLAN YOUR INVESTMENT

Your total investment of time in relationship building will depend on your role in your organization. If you are the primary person responsible for sales in your organization, you likely already have measurable goals for how many customer contacts you make every week. For those who don't have primary sales responsibility, it may be a new concept to set goals for relationship building. Sales is only one part of building business relationships. As a leader, I know that I am the face of my organization, and the relationships I build are key to its success. You may already spend time building relationships on behalf of your organization. For example, if you are a CEO, your chief sales officer may bring you into key customer appointments. If you are the executive director or president of a nonprofit organization, you are likely spending a significant portion of your time meeting with major donors.

Whatever your role in your organization, now that you have identified who you want to build better relationships with, it is time to decide how much time you will invest in doing so. I call it an investment because the time that you spend building relationships will have a direct impact on the success of your organization. Like all your investments, both the activity and the results of the activity can be measured. In my twenty-plus years of owning a business, I have observed that there is a direct correlation between the number of networking meetings I have on my calendar and the performance of the business. Because I track all of my networking activity, I have the data to show this return on investment.

You may already be spending as much time as you can making connections. This is fine. The point of this step is to be intentional in the time you spend. If you are already maximizing the relationship-building time on your calendar, you do not need to add more activity. Your goal will be to balance your time among your Key Relationship types so that you are spending your best and most focused time with those relationships that are most important to you.

Setting a weekly activity goal helps encourage you to keep working at relationships. It reminds you that networking is important, and this time is an important investment in building your business. Your weekly activity goal is something you can hold yourself accountable to, and it becomes a benchmark for you to measure progress toward your goal of better relationships.

I have found there are two components to planning an investment in relationship building. The first is deciding how much time to spend on relationships. It should not be so much that you don't have time to manage your other responsibilities. It should also not be so much time that you can't manage the tasks and follow-through that come out of your relationship connections.

The second is deciding how much of that time to spend on each of your Key Relationship types, and how to make those decisions quickly and efficiently so that your Relationship Code makes you better at building relationships, not burdened by keeping up a system.

If your calendar is already full of meetings, you may want to use this opportunity to rebalance the types of meetings you are doing. Are they all internal meetings? Could some of that time be better spent expanding your external relationships? After looking at your calendar, you may decide that you are spending time with too many of the wrong types of people. Once you have identified your Key Relationship types, you may find that you are over-invested in the kinds of people who are not going to get you to your relationship goals.

In 2006 Michael Porter and Nitin Nohria launched a study of how CEO's spend their time. In 2018 they published results of this longitudinal study in the Harvard Business Review. "On average, the leaders in our study had 37 meetings of assorted lengths in any given week and spent 72% of their total work time in meetings."[1]

According to Dr. Ivan Misner, who is considered the father of modern networking and the founder of BNI, the largest business network organization in the world, the average successful business networker spends about 6.3 hours per week networking. However, he also says that the ideal time is about ten hours per week.[2]

How do I decide how much time to spend in relationship-building meetings every week? Mostly by trial and error, I have learned that scheduling three meetings per day is optimum for me. It allows me enough time to follow up with tasks that the meetings generate and enough time for the focused writing and creative work that my role requires. These three meetings per day include meetings with my internal team, with current clients, and meetings that expand and cultivate my relationship network. It is important to note that this does not include asynchronous contact points like email messages, voice mails, text messages, and social media contacts, such as LinkedIn. Asynchronous connections are additional contact points that support the total relationship-building efforts.

The second part of planning your relationship investment is to decide how much time, or how many meetings, to devote to each of your Key Relationship types. If you have identified three types of key relationships, you will want to make sure that you are balancing your meeting capacity every week so that you are devoting most of your time to your most important relationships—those whom you have designated as your highest priority Key Relationship type.

How you divide your time between your highest priority Key Relationship types will vary depending on how many you have, and if they are of equal priority. One method is to give equal time to each of your priority relationship types. Another method is the 3-2-1 ratio. This method allots more time to the top Key Relationship types. For every six meetings or phone connections you schedule, three of them will be with your top Key Relationship type, two of them will be with your second-priority Key Relationship type, and one of them will be with your third most important Key Relationship type. This ensures that your time is balanced and in line with your priorities.

However, this can also be somewhat unwieldy in practice. It sounds good on paper, but when I am trying to get my in-box to zero and have multiple meeting requests to get through in a short period of time, I don't want to be slowed down by going back to my calendar and counting every meeting and phone call to figure out how many of a specific type of connections I have made in the week. After all, the point of a good Relationship Code is to make you more efficient at networking and meeting relationship goals. It is not supposed to be an additional burden on your time.

So I have created a short-cut to make quick decisions to balance my Key Relationship types by scheduling meetings with my top-priority Key Relationships any week in the month. Then, I limit my second highest Key Relationship type to weeks two through four of the month, and my third highest Key Relationship type to the third and fourth weeks of the month. This means that I don't have to stop and count before scheduling a meeting or call. If a lower priority type of person wants to meet, I have three weeks of the month available to meet with them. But if a top-priority person wants to meet, any week of the month is available for them.

But how do you know how much time to devote to people you already know and to expanding your network to include new people? This is something that I struggled with early in my career. One thing that helped me think through this was to place a priority on existing relationships. Also, at least once a month, I attend an event or put myself in a place where I can meet new people who fit within my Key Relationship types.

CHAPTER 8

PUT PEOPLE FIRST

" I t's my job to ask. It's their job to say no."
In the *The Speed of Trust* by Steven R. Covey, he explains that relationships are built on trust, and the greater the trust, the faster the relationship will yield benefits for both of those involved: "When trust goes up, speed will also go up and costs will go down." One of the key building blocks of trust, according to Covey's research, is that people believe you have their best interests at heart.[1]

The goal of a Relationship Code is to build relationships that are founded on mutual trust and mutual benefit. It is never about seeing how much you can get from the other person. We build great relationships by demonstrating to the other person we are worthy of their trust. Therefore every good Relationship Code will include an intentionality about communicating to the other person that we are we are putting them at the center of the relationship.

One of the first ways you can do this in a relationship is to use the other person's preferred method of communication when you reach out to them. There is a concept called "mirroring" in psychology. According to Wikipedia, "mirroring" is the behavior in which one person unconsciously imitates the gesture, speech pattern, or attitude of another. Mirroring often occurs in social situations, particularly in the company of close friends or family.[2] We often do it without even thinking about it.

We can apply this concept of mirroring in the Relationship Code in that we match whatever communication method the other person prefers, whether that be phone, email, text messaging, or even smoke signal! This keeps the other person in their comfort zone and subtly communicates to them that you are paying attention and their preferences matter to you.

I have found that it may take some trial and error to find what someone's communication preference is. If someone reaches out to you via one method, for example, try to stay with that method until they switch to another. If you are reaching out to them first, try one method and then try something else if you don't hear from them. If you are trying to reach someone that you already have a relationship with but they are not responding, switch methods until you find what they do respond to.

Always try to give people the benefit of the doubt. Emails do get lost in cyberspace. Voice mails accidentally get erased. We all have the best intentions of responding to all of our LinkedIn messages. Sometimes life gets in the way and we forget to respond, if even we intended to, even if we genuinely like the person who is trying to reach us. We are all overwhelmed by too much information and too many messages coming at us.

Recently, the concept of "ghosting" has become a popular topic. According to Wikipedia, "Ghosting is breaking off a relationship by stopping all communication and contact with the partner without any apparent warning or justification, as well as ignoring the partner's attempts to reach out or communicate. The term originated in the mid-2000s."[3] Unfortunately, ghosting has made its way into business relationships. More likely, ghosting has existed in sales relationships for many years, and it is now spilling over into our personal relationships. Every salesperson I know can tell tales of the potential client who was eager to talk about a sale but then disappeared into thin air after he or she had put many hours into building the relationship.

Having a solid, intentional Relationship Code can help take the emotion out of these situations by giving us some ground rules for how to deal with someone who is ghosting us. Of course, we should never take it personally. One of our favorite sayings at Outsight is, "It's our job to ask. It's their job to say no." The only side of the relationship you can control is your side. If someone chooses not to respond, that is their responsibility. If you make an effort to reach out, and if you communicate the value that you can bring to a relationship and someone is still ignoring you, then a Relationship Code will provide a guideline for how long to keep trying and when to move on.

Some people I know have a "three strikes and you are out," relationship rule. If they have tried to reach someone three times in at least two different ways and the other person has not responded, they stopped trying and assume that person is not interested.

I think that the speed and volume of communications has increased significantly in the last few years, and that means you are competing for attention with many more messages than you ever have before. So I give people the benefit of the doubt longer than I might have ten years ago. Also, I use more varied communication types than I might have in the past. Rather than just switching between phone and email, I also use LinkedIn messaging and text message if I have their cell phone. And I also like sending a hand-written note.

The point is not to stop communicating altogether just because someone does not respond; instead, shift your communication methods and slow down the frequency with which you communicate. All relationships have a velocity to them. Essentially, when someone doesn't respond, it is a definite signal that the velocity of the relationship has slowed down considerably, and it is wise to match that velocity accordingly.

The second way of putting people first is to always connect based on their primary interests. One reason people don't respond to a communication is that whatever you are offering is of no interest or relevance to them. In this crowded, busy world, if you are not providing something of real value, something that will help solve a real and immediate challenge, then the other person is completely justified in not responding to you. I know that sounds harsh, but it is our responsibility to bring something of value to every relationship. And if you are not doing that, or if you haven't made the value clear to the other person, you can't expect a response from them. Don't take it personally, but do try to learn from every situation. Sometimes, things just aren't a good fit. Not everyone is going to like you or want to strike up a business relationship with you. It's your job to ask. It's their job to say no. And that's okay.

This is especially true, I believe, of business relationships. You absolutely need to understand what people care about to put their interests first. What are they working on? What are their goals? What gets them out of bed in the morning? What does the world most need them to do? Find these things out and connect on the things that matter most to the other person.

The third way to put people first in the relationship is to know how you can be helpful to them. It is easy to know how someone can be helpful to us. That is typically why you reach out to new business contacts. They have something you need or want, whether it is a resource, a business connection, or influence. We are wired to put ourselves at the center of every interaction.

We all know that people are preoccupied with themselves. We spend a lot of time talking about ourselves in conversation, posting about ourselves on social media, and even thinking about ourselves when we should be paying attention to something else. In a study at Dartmouth, neuroscientists Meghan Meyer and Matt Lieberman (UCLA) revealed a brain mechanism that biases people toward self-focus, providing the first neural explanation of why people frequently circle back to themselves. The Default Mode Network, or what our brains are doing when we are not doing anything else, activates the same area of the brain that processes self-reflection.[4] The default mode network (DMN) is a system of connected brain areas that show increased activity when a person is not focused on what is happening around them. In other words, our brain's "default mode" is to think about ourselves.

Therefore we can expect that the other person we are reaching out to will also be thinking about their own interests and their own goals. We can also expect that if we understand how we can be helpful to them, and we start the relationship there, the chance that they will respond to us will be much higher.

But it isn't just about the initial contact. Nor is it about manipulating people into doing something we want them to do. Genuine, trusting business relationships are built on mutual benefit. So whether you are reaching out for the first time or the one hundred fifty-first time, always know how you can be helpful to the person to whom you are reaching out.

The People First exercise is a great way to challenge your knowledge about your relationships. Select five contacts in your network and see how many of the following questions you can answer about each one. To make it even more challenging, select five contacts at random from your database (www.random.org is a great tool for this).

1. Who introduced you to this person?
2. What is their favorite way to communicate?
3. What is their superpower, the one thing someone should pay them one million dollars to do?
4. What is their "big idea," the one concept or goal that motivates all of their work?
5. What do they need most from you?

Putting people first means that you are paying attention to how they want to connect, what drives their work, and why they might want to connect. It also helps you provide value in every relationship connection.

CHAPTER 9

START WITH A YES

Conventional wisdom says that when we are networking, we will first do people a favor, then they will feel obligated to repay us when we need something from them. I have always been rather uncomfortable with that approach. First, I think most people will see right through that and wonder what I am up to, or why I am being so nice. Call me cynical. Second, it has always felt weird to want people to feel indebted to me so that they have to do something for me to pay me back. I don't want people to feel obligated to me and grudgingly return a favor so they can get out from that indebtedness. I would much rather that they feel like we are engaged in a mutually beneficial relationship. That they trust that whenever possible I will help them, and if it is within their power, they will help me. Not out of obligation, but out of mutual respect and a desire to be helpful. I believe a rising tide raises all boats and that the universe will ultimately return seven-fold what we have given to others. I don't want to be keeping that kind of score in every relationship. It's important to keep data about relationships, but not that kind of data.

Human beings are hardwired to help each other. According to an article in *Psychology Today*, we are happier when we help others. In one study cited in the article, participants were approached on the street after parking their cars. They were given a few quarters by a research assistant and were asked to either feed their own parking meters or the meters of an adjacent car. The researchers then asked participants how happy they felt. Interestingly, people who fed others' meters showed a greater boost in happiness than those who fed their own meters, despite not knowing who they were helping.[1]

Research as early as the 1960s bears this out, saying that when we do someone a favor, our opinion of that person increases. Regardless of what we thought of them before, we will think more highly of them after we do them a favor.[2] Whether this is because we are wired to help, or because our brains must reconcile the cognitive dissonance of doing something nice for someone we don't like, the result is the same. When we do a favor for someone, even a small favor, we end up liking the person more.

This is known in psychology as the Ben Franklin Effect. It was named for Benjamin Franklin because Franklin described how he dealt with the animosity of a rival legislator. After hearing that his rival had a rare book in his library, Franklin wrote to his rival and asked whether he could borrow the book for a few days. The rival agreed, and a week later Franklin returned the book with a letter expressing how much he liked it. The next time the two met, Franklin's rival spoke to him with great civility and showed a willingness to help him in other matters, leading the two men to become good friends. Franklin consequently referred to this effect as an old axiom, stating that, "He that has once done you a kindness will be more ready to do you another, than he whom you yourself have obliged."[3]

What I have learned in putting this principal into practice is that it is important to think carefully about what I am asking people to do for me. There are two rules that I apply. First, the request must be small. Second, the request must be something that is easy for the other person to say yes to. If you ask for something big or something difficult right away, you have crossed the line and are no longer putting the other person first.

Relationship building is asking people for a series of small "yesses." Each yes is a progression in the relationship. Each yes brings us closer together in a mutual purpose. The very act of asking for a meeting is asking the other person to say yes to something, for example.

One of my favorite stories in the Bible is the story of Queen Esther. When Esther and the Jewish people were in danger of being annihilated, Queen Esther was in a position to do something about it. However, no one could approach the king without risking death. Just being in his presence uninvited was a risky undertaking, and the previous queen had learned that lesson the hard way. Asking for the change of a royal decree was a significant ask.

So Esther used a series of smaller yesses to work up to the big ask. Her first request was showing up uninvited. When the king received her, she invited him to a banquet. That was easy for the king to say yes to. Her next request was an invitation to another banquet, again something the king could easily say yes to. Eventually, Esther asked the king to intervene on behalf of her people, and he did so. A big yes.

It is helpful to have a list of easy yesses ready to go when you need them. Of course, not all of these apply to every situation, and you will want to tailor your asks to the specific situation.

Here is a beginning list I have used. Some of them are bigger than others, and they are in no particular order.

- Ask for an introduction to someone they know.
- Ask if you can use their name to reach out to someone they know.
- Ask who else you should be talking to about a subject.
- Ask them to read something you wrote (a short piece, like a blog post) and give you feedback on it.

- Ask their opinion on a topic they are interested in.
- Ask if you can interview them for something you are writing.
- Ask to borrow a book (a la Ben Franklin).
- Invite them to coffee.
- Ask them to look at your website and give you feedback on it.
- Ask them what they would recommend when making a choice. (Remember, small is good. This could be asking what entree they would order at a restaurant.)
- Ask them for advice on a business decision you will be making.
- Ask them to send you a link to something they referenced in conversation.

This is just a short list. There are hundreds of ways that you can ask small yesses, things that are easy for people to agree to. Do you have more ideas? Go to www.kayedwardsauthor.com and share your ideas.

The important part of all of this is to make sure whatever you are asking is small and something that is easy for the other person to do; something they are interested in.

The other important thing to remember is to say, "Thank you." Always. Always. Always say thank you when people do something for you, no matter how small. I am a big fan of the handwritten thank-you note. It doesn't matter what you say. It doesn't matter if your handwriting isn't the best. Mine is terrible. It matters that you took the time to write out a thank-you note and put it in the mail. Don't use a pre-printed thank-you card. Write something from your heart. Even a single sentence is acceptable. It's the least you can do for someone who has graciously said yes to your request.

My last word of advice on starting with a yes is to *do what you say you will do*. Once you get in the habit of asking for small yesses, you will notice two things. First, you will notice that you become more comfortable with asking. Second, you will notice how often others are asking you to say yes to their small requests. Overall, you will notice how much fun it is to be helpful to others.

CHAPTER 10

LEARNING THE RELATIONSHIP DANCE

R elationships are like a dance. They are constantly moving. They are never static. Even business relationships are like a dance. Both partners have a role in the relationship, and both need to recognize that you can't do the same step over and over again and expect a great result.

While we start the relationship by asking for a small yes, or a series of small yesses, there is more to building trust than this. There are three things that we do in a relationship: we are either asking the other person for something, we are listening to them, or we are creating value for the other person. In the previous step, we learned that *asking* means asking someone to do something for us, even if it's something small.

Listening is a different kind of asking. It means being open and receptive to the other person's ideas and thoughts. It is a learning stance. It is asking questions with the goal of hearing what the other person has to say, what is on their mind and on their heart, and learning more about them. It is a completely open and giving posture toward the other person. It is one of the most difficult things we can do for someone, particularly in a business relationship, because it means subjugating our ego and our needs in favor of the other person for a period while we listen, absorb the information, and offer our presence.

Why is this important? Because to have a meaningful business relationship, we need to understand the other person so well that we know their needs, their frustrations, their hopes, their dreams, what they are doing to fulfill those hopes and dreams, and what is standing in their way. It is the only way to bring value to a business relationship in the long term. We can fake a good business relationship for a while, but unless we spend significant time listening, we can't sustain a mutually beneficial relationship over the long term.

This type of listening is common in market research, where the researcher is asked to conduct in-depth interviews or facilitate focus groups and be completely neutral in the process to avoid biasing the data. Researchers are trained to ask questions in a neutral way and to avoid responding in any way that suggests that an answer is either right or wrong, allowing the research subjects to pursue their own thoughts with as little intervention from the interviewer as possible.

While this is a bit extreme for the average business conversation, it does provide great training for listening in any kind of relationship. The most relevant aspects of this listening strategy are to be focused completely on the other person. What are they trying to say? What's important to them? What do they love? What do they hate?

In *What Customers Crave* by Nicholas J. Webb, he asks readers to think about what their customers love and what they hate.[1] It is in these passionate polar opposites that we begin to understand what drives people, and if we understand what drives them, we can begin to understand how we can add value to the relationship.

What kinds of questions can we ask that put others at the center of the relationship and uncover what they care about? Here are some questions I like that are completely business-appropriate and won't be perceived as too personal, but still cut through the clutter and ask people to respond with more than surface-level answers. They are not your typical meeting questions, which means that people must stop and think before they answer.

- What does the world most need you to do?
- What is your greatest hope for your organization in the next five years?
- What is taking most of your focus this year?
- What one thing would make your organization more effective?
- What have you tried already, and what did you like or not like about doing that?
- What is the most important thing you have learned in the last year?

Good questions are like a gift we give to the people we interact with. They are the key to unlocking what is most important for people. Which brings us to the third way we interact with people: we add value. We bless them with things that they need from us and the things that they value about us. This is an important part of the relationship because it means it is no longer a one-way relationship. It is not about what we can take from someone; it is about what we contribute to someone. The relationship dance is all about balancing the time you spend in each type of interaction so that it is never one-sided; sometimes you are asking and sometimes you are giving, and you are always paying attention to where you are in the relationship.

When you put together your Key Relationship Chart, you listed the types of people who benefit from the work that your organization does. No matter what you do or the size of your organization, there are a significant number of people who benefit from the work that you and your organization do. When you do it well, you are adding value to your constituents, your customers, and all your stakeholders.

There are many other ways that you can add value to those you network with. The list looks a lot like the ways that you can ask people to do things for you. Here are some of my favorite ways to add value:

- Make an introduction to someone who is interested in what they are interested in.
- Look for work opportunities for those who are looking for a new position.
- Send a note of encouragement.
- Ask a great question that provokes deep thought. Not a question that is for us to learn from, but to spark new thinking for them. They don't even need to answer the question.
- Share an idea from a different network or industry that they might not have come across.
- Lighten their day with humor. (I once sent a video of baby goats wearing pajamas to a client. I think she enjoyed it.)
- Send an article that would be of interest to them.

There are so many ways to add value. This is just the tip of the iceberg. Use your creativity and create your own list of ways to add value to people in your network.

DISCERN WHEN YOU CAN'T
ADD VALUE

Most of the relationship giants I spoke with place a high priority on serving others through their relationship-building practices. The primary question they ask themselves when meeting someone new is, "How can I serve the person I am meeting today?" rather than, "How can this person serve me?" One individual described this as a discernment process. He is always asking himself if he is focused on meeting people who he can serve disproportionately well.

These networkers believe that if they can't add value to a relationship, they are wasting their own and the other person's time and see it as an act of generosity to not take a second meeting. Their goal is to be professional and polite, and part of that professionalism is to recognize that the other person would be better served spending their time networking with somebody else. Many say their practice is to look for someone else in their network who can better serve the person reaching out to them. But if that doesn't exist, they are quick to say so and let the other person move on.

A good Relationship Code will help you keep an appropriate balance in your business relationships, balancing asking, listening, and adding value in a way that feels natural and keeps the relationship from being one-sided. A good balance is one part asking, two parts listening, and three parts adding value. There is no perfect order to this, but it is helpful to pay attention and track where you are in every relationship so that you can keep these well-balanced. For example, if the last time you reached out to someone was with a request for an introduction, make sure that the next interaction with that person is either listening or adding value.

How do you keep track? Make a note on every meeting or phone call appointment in your CRM system that tells you the primary purpose of the connection—asking, listening, or adding value. It becomes a habit that is easy to do while scheduling contacts in your calendar.

Now it's your turn. Go back to the People First form and complete the rest of it. For each person you included on the form, list at least one ask, two listening questions, and three ways that you can add value to this individual.

How difficult was that? Need more ideas for any of the parts of the relationship dance? Go to www.kayedwardsauthor.com to see more ideas in each area. Send us your favorite ones, and let us know how it is going. We'd love to hear your stories.

CHAPTER 11

USE VELOCITY STRATEGICALLY

A re we there yet?

Just like relationships are a dance, relationships vary in their pace. They speed up and they slow down. This is natural and to be expected. We could not sustain relationships if they were always moving along at the same intensity. Even our closest personal relationships, our relationship with our spouse or significant other, ebb and flow. They change over time.

Business relationships in particular often go through cycles of intensity. There are times in business relationships where we are working very intensely together toward a common goal. Perhaps it is a team at your organization that is working on a project. Or it may be a project with a client that you are working on for a short period of time. Part of what makes the relationship so strong in those situations is that we are creating something together, we are working toward a common goal, and we have a shared vision for what we want to accomplish.

However, there comes a time when the creation phase is over, and the team needs to take the idea or the new product to the marketplace, or to the rest of the organization. This is where the dynamics of the relationship change from the intense, working-together stage to the stage in which we bring it out to our broader network and "socialize" the idea or concept. It is in this stage that the relationship often becomes less intense. This happens because each of the people on the team are focused elsewhere. They are focused on bringing the new product or idea into a new network, and there is less time and energy focused on the relationship that created the product or idea in the first place. This is when relationship velocity slows down.

In the consulting world, this happens over and over again with each new client engagement. Even in long-term engagements over multiple years, there is a natural ebb and flow to the relationship. It may be more subtle, but it still happens.

In many cases, the cycle repeats itself within the same relationship. The team comes back together for the next project, or the client calls again to do the next phase of work. But it doesn't always work that way. Sometimes there is no reason to come back together, and the velocity of the relationship continues to slow down until one party or the other does something to increase the speed. I have found that the secret ingredient to spark velocity is not just shared interest, but a shared cause, something that both parties are working together to create. In practice, velocity in a relationship cycle looks something like this.

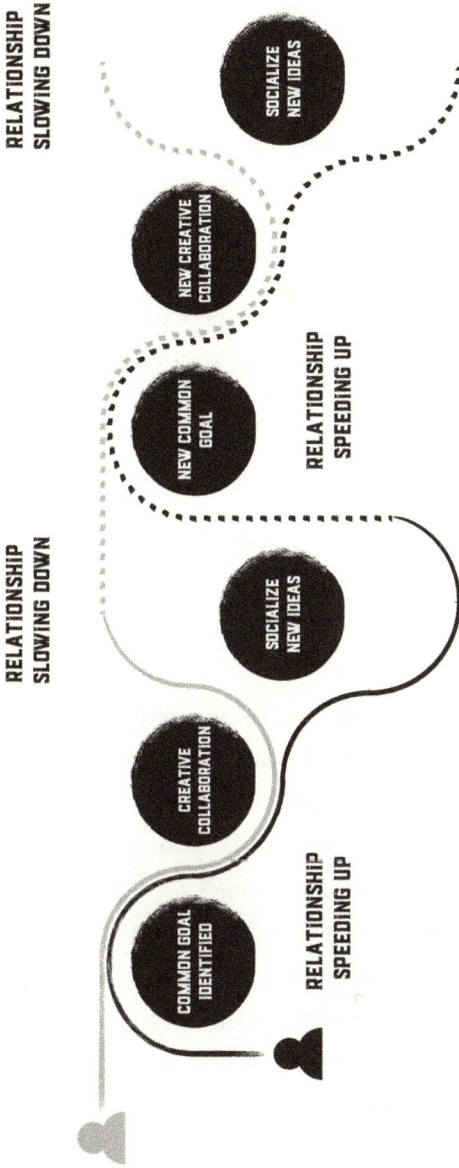

In managing a business network, it is vital to understand the concept of velocity and to know whether or not a given relationship is speeding up or slowing down. Then you can time connections based on which direction the relationship is headed. Why is this important? Because if the relationship is naturally slowing down and you try to connect too often, you run the risk of being annoying. And if the relationship is speeding up and you don't respond often enough, you run the risk of being the one who drops the proverbial relationship ball.

Velocity is directly correlated to joint activity. In other words, if there is something meaningful for two people to do together, the relationship will speed up. If there is nothing for two people to do together, the relationship will slow down. So it's important to know where you are in that cycle in every relationship.

How do you use velocity strategically in your business relationships? Be aware of the current velocity of the relationship, and be intentional about responding to the velocity. It speeds up when there is something you can do together ,and it slows down when there isn't.

That doesn't mean we are completely at the mercy of some unknown forces of velocity working on our relationships. There are two people who control the relationship: you and the other person. That means you have half of the power to speed things up and slow things down. That means half of the velocity equation is your responsibility.

So what can you do with your half of the velocity equation? You can recognize what is happening with the velocity of each relationship you are in. There are some pretty easy clues that I look for:

1. Are we working on something together? (Speeding up)
2. Is the time between connections getting shorter? (Speeding up)
3. Is the time between connections getting longer? (Slowing down)
4. Does the other person reach out to me first? (Speeding up)

5. Am I always the one to initiate a contact? (Slowing down)
6. Has the other person asked me for something? (Speeding up)
7. Am I the one who is asking them for something? (Slowing down)
8. Has the other person not responded to a contact point via email, phone, text, etc.? (Slowing down)
9. At the end of the meeting or phone call, are there specific next steps that we have both committed to? (Speeding up)
10. At the end of the meeting or phone call, did we struggle to figure out what the next step was, or did we say something like, "We should get together again sometime?" (Slowing down)

Once you start looking for velocity, it's pretty easy to spot. If you are struggling with expanding your network, reading the velocity clues and following up on them will help to grow your network in a way that respects the status of each relationship and will feel more natural and comfortable for both you and the people you are connecting with.

To use velocity wisely, pay attention to where you are and plan your next step with the connection accordingly. For example, at the end of every meeting, ask yourself, "Is this relationship speeding up or is it slowing down?" If it is speeding up it, typically means you named some specific next steps and gave a timeline to check back. Use that information to schedule the next step on your calendar.

If for some reason you did not set any tasks or any schedule to check in again, you can decide the velocity based on some other factor. Maybe you are working on something together, but you didn't stop to identify specific next steps. The relationship is still speeding up, but it is up to you to make sure the next step happens. Take the initiative and schedule that on your calendar.

Or maybe you didn't name any next steps because you couldn't think of anything to do together. But you still like each other and wish there was something to do together. In that case, the relationship is probably slowing down. Or, if it is a first meeting, the relationship may never find a way to get off the ground, which means any early velocity it had is probably now slowing down already. In cases like these, I will still schedule a follow-up connection in my calendar, but I will schedule it for later and intentionally lengthen the time until the next connection.

If you are not happy that a relationship seems to be slowing down, you can create a velocity intervention. Remember, you have control over your half of the velocity equation. Velocity is directly correlated to work that you do with someone else to reach a common goal. If you want to create a velocity intervention and speed up a relationship because you see potential in it, go back to Step 4 in the Relationship Code Game Plan and ask the other person for a small yes. It really doesn't matter how small it is. The point is to create something for the two of you to do together, some small commonality that may serve to speed up the relationship once again.

One of my favorite velocity interventions is my Very Random Database Project. I began this project many years ago as I looked through my database and realized that I had neglected relationships. I had unintentionally let them slip away over the years. There were many people with whom I had had wonderful working relationships over twenty-five years of my consulting career. But now I struggled with how to reconnect. How do you pick up the phone ten years after a project and say, "Hey, that was great. Can we do it again?"

So I created the Very Random Database Project to do just that. Every day, I pick one name out of my database at random and reach out to that person and ask them a question. Every year I pick a different question, something that allows people to stop and think deeply about their work. If people respond, I ask their permission to post their reply on the Very Random Database Project gallery page on our website. Many people respond. Many people do not. Either is okay with me. It gives us something small to do together, some shared purpose that makes reaching out easier, even if it has been many years. It gives me a way to potentially reignite the velocity in relationships that have slowed down to the point of being almost nonexistent. Or it can reinforce an already strong connection. It doesn't matter that the cause of answering a question is small. It is something we are engaging in together. Even for those who don't respond, I now have a clearer sense of the velocity of the relationship and can plan accordingly.

This is just one example of restarting the velocity of a relationship in a positive direction. Now it's your turn. Go back to the People First Form, and for each person on the list decide which direction the velocity of the relationship is going. Is it speeding up? Is it slowing down? If it is speeding up, check the up arrow, and next to it write down the common cause or project that you are working on together. Can't think of one? Maybe the relationship is not speeding up after all. Would you like to change the velocity? Think of some small thing you can ask for, write it down, and write down the date you will do it. If the relationship is truly slowing down, check the down arrow. The next step is to decide if you want to change that. If you do, write down what you will do and when you will do it. Then schedule that on your calendar.

You are now using velocity strategically.

CHAPTER 12

MAKE ROOM FOR ADVENTURE

S urprise Me!

By now you are well on your way to Relationship Code success. You have identified your Key Relationship types, you have planned your relationship-building time investment, and you have strategies to start building relationships effectively. At this point you may be wondering what to do when you get one too many "coffee meeting" requests, or what happens to people who don't fall into one of your Key Relationship type categories. What do you do with the request that comes out of the blue from someone you don't know and doesn't really look like someone who can benefit you or your organization?

One of the best parts of having a good Relationship Code is that it allows you to make room for adventure. Because you are no longer guessing about the best relationship strategy and are no longer overwhelmed by haphazard networking activity, you can make room for a few serendipitous appointments on your calendar every month.

At Outsight we call these mystery people, and I reserve a few appointment slots for them because I never know how it will turn out.

Sometimes we simply have a good cup of coffee and a good conversation. Sometimes not. And sometimes it turns out that the person who didn't look like a good fit on paper is working on something very interesting, very exciting, and very much in line with our mission and vision. Or we can connect them to someone in our network who would benefit from knowing them and what they are working on.

One of the delights of becoming a great networker is that an increasing number of people will reach out to you asking for those coffee meetings. Because you intentionally make room for these types of connections, you can sometimes say yes, and if you need to say no because there are too many of them already on your calendar, you don't need to feel obligated or guilty. It is all about the balance.

In your Relationship Code, the total number of mystery dates you carve out is completely up to you. It may be one a quarter. It may be one a week. The point is that you leave at least some connections open for God, the universe, karma, or whatever you prefer to call it to bring unexpected blessings into your life. If nothing else, you will have some interesting stories to tell and will meet some good people along the way.

TOOLS THEY RELY ON

Some of the relationship giants I interviewed rely on specific tools that help them manage the process of building business relationships. Because each of these individuals are super-networkers, they employ tools to help them manage their networking time without becoming overwhelmed by the process.

Some of my favorites include:

A defined rhythm for how they connect to people. Whether they are initiating the contact or whether they are following up after a first meeting, a number of interviewees shared that they have a specific sequence of emails, phone calls, and text messages they employ. If they get to the end of the sequence and have not heard back from an individual, they stop trying. The exact combination and total number of contacts varies from one interviewee to another, but this "shorthand" of touch points provides a guide that tells them when it is time to move on.

A "cheat sheet" of conversation starters and topics to check in on when meeting with someone for the second time. According to one interviewee, as long as your intentions are sincere, having a plan going into a networking meeting makes a lot of sense.

A set of email templates for common messages. One interviewee has created a set of email templates that address the things he commonly communicates about. He can quickly pull up the appropriate email template, modify it for the situation, and send it out. This saves him a great deal of time managing emails, especially emails to follow up on networking meetings.

A go-to location for meetings. Another interviewee said he meets everyone at the same coffee shop to save time and effort. This allows him to schedule multiple networking meetings in a day without taking time to drive from one place to another.

CHAPTER 13

DECIDE WHEN TO LET GO

66 This just isn't working for me anymore."

The last step in creating your Relationship Code game plan is to decide when you will truly let a relationship go. How many times will you reach out before you take someone off your contact list? What are the clues that the relationship is over? What kind of relationship boundaries will you set? What happens when someone retires? What happens when someone dies?

All of these are important questions to consider when establishing your networking practices. At first glance, some of these questions might seem silly. Of course, the relationship is over when someone dies, for example. And everyone has people in their lives who have become toxic, who have tried too many times to overstep appropriate boundaries, and who we are happy to walk away from.

A good Relationship Code will provide guidelines to know when to let go in each situation, and those guidelines will be based on your unique situation, not anyone else's. What are the situations in which you will need to make a decision about letting go? Here is a list of common ones I have experienced.

- Someone is not responding to your attempts to make contact.
- Someone has unsubscribed from your email list.
- Someone has directly told you they are not interested in your products or services.
- You have submitted a proposal, and the organization declines to buy your products or services.
- Someone has done something that is contrary to your personal or organizational values.
- You have had a disagreement with someone.
- Someone has retired.
- Someone has died.

Each of these situations calls for a specific decision about how you are going to respond. Each of these situations is slightly different, and different people will handle them differently, depending on their relationship style and goals. However, there are specific questions I have asked myself in each of these situations that have helped me determine what my Relationship Code is suggesting to do next.

1. *Someone is not responding to your attempts to make contact.* In this case, you have made all of the efforts that you had planned earlier, including switching the ways in which you make contact, making sure you are offering something of value, putting the other person at the center of the relationship, and knowing what the other person is interested in. And, for whatever reason, they have simply not responded. Ask yourself the following questions.

    a. What is the potential payoff if this person does eventually respond?

b.   Do I need to shift the value I am bringing?

c.   Could someone else make an introduction for me?

d.   Is there someone else who could bring an equal or higher value to my network?

e.   Is pursuing this person keeping me from reaching out to other, more valuable connections?

If, as you answer the first three questions, you think there are still some strategies to be tried, go for it. If the answer to the last two questions is yes, you are likely better off shifting your attention to other connections. You then have several options. You could keep them on your list and adopt a very low-key, slow-velocity approach of keeping in touch. For example, you could put them on your general newsletter list and take them off your personal contact list. Remember Dunbar's Number here. You don't want to spend your personal networking time on someone who is not going to respond. Eventually, if they reach out to you, you can change their status and your focus on them.

Or you could continue to reach out but on a much slower schedule, say once every year or so, and until they specifically tell you to stop contacting them, or until they respond. All of this will depend on your assessment of whether or not you can add value to this person's business life. Remember, it is about adding value to them first before you think about what value they can bring to you. Because they will only respond if they believe that you have something of value to add to their world.

2.   *Someone has unsubscribed from your mailing list.* This is a tricky one because you don't know if they are completely uninterested in you as a person and what your organization has to offer, or if they simply have an overwhelmed email inbox. In this case, ask yourself these questions:

a.   Do I have a personal relationship with this person?

    b.   If I met this person on the street, would I have something to talk about that this person is interested in?

    c.   If I reached out to this person via a more personal connection method, such as phone or email, would they respond?

    d.   Do I even have their phone number?

First, if someone unsubscribes from your mass email list, you *must delete* them from your mass email list. To do otherwise is illegal and puts you at risk of being blocked from email systems as a spammer. Do not be tempted to keep them on your list. But do give yourself permission to not take it personally. My best strategy is to sigh and say, "Oh well," and then think about all of the new opportunities that will present themselves in the future.

Second, decide if you will take them off of your personal contact list as well. It comes down to how many other contacts you have and if pursuing this relationship will distract you from other, potentially more favorable ones.

3.   *Someone has directly told you they are not interest in your products or services.* First, take a deep breath and appreciate that someone has taken the time to be honest with you. It is a rare gift. Celebrate that and thank them for their honesty. They have just saved you a great deal of time and effort. If you believe there is still value to the relationship, outside of a direct client/customer transaction, you may want to keep them on your list and put them on a slow-velocity relationship schedule, reaching out once a year or so, and only with something that you know they will value, never with a sales pitch. People with this degree of candor and forthrightness are rare, and you may want to

stay in touch with someone like that. If you believe there is no values alignment, my best advice is to wish them well and take them off all of your lists.

4. *You have submitted a proposal, and the organization has declined to buy your product or services.* Ouch, that hurts. Take a deep breath and remember not to take it personally. There are so many reasons why these things happen. Then ask yourself these questions:

   a. Do you know the real reason why the organization said no?

   b. Does the relationship feel like a good values alignment for your organization? (See the chapter on the relationship formula for a reminder of what this looks like.)

   c. Have they suggested that you keep in touch?

If you suspect you don't know the *real* reason (not just the reason they stated) they said no to your proposal, go back and ask. Ask them to be brutally honest, and say that you really want to learn from this situation. If it is truly about something beyond your control and not about the values fit with the leadership of the organization, keep them on your list. Decide how and how often you will stay in touch, and then celebrate because sometimes no is the first step on the way to yes. There was obviously something about the relationship that led to the request for a proposal in the first place.

A word of caution for consultants. In consulting there is something we call the "Go Away Proposal." Do not be fooled by these. This is not a step toward a great relationship. This is a giant leap away from relationship. A Go Away Proposal happens when a potential client says, early in the relationship, "Send me a proposal." Do not, under any circumstance, agree with this request. They don't really mean it. What they really mean is, "I am trying to find a way to get rid of you. I will get your proposal and delete it from my inbox and never think about you again."

How do you know when a request for a proposal is legitimate? I never write a proposal unless three things have happened in relationship conversations with the potential client. 1) We have agreed on what problem they need to solve. 2) We have agreed verbally on the appropriate approach to solve their problem. 3) We have agreed on the value of solving the problem for the business and have discussed a ballpark fee for our services. Then, and only then, will I take the time to write the proposal and put together a budget for our work. Then, and only then, do I know that the leader is serious about engaging us to work with them.

5. *Someone has done something that is contrary to your organizational or personal values.* This is also tricky because it depends on whether this is a pattern or an outlier. If someone made a mistake and is willing to own up to that, they deserve another chance. If someone is going to continue to behave in ways that violate your values, it is time to take them off your list. Ask yourself these questions:

    a. Was it an honest mistake?
    b. Has this person done something similar before, either to you or to someone else you know?
    c. Did the person's actions hurt one of your team members?

I am willing to forgive an awful lot from people, but I am a big stickler when it comes to the Outsight core values. If someone goes against our values, and especially if someone takes advantage of one of my teams, I am likely to take them off of our list. Fortunately, it has only happened a handful of times in my career.

What are some examples of things that caused me to take someone off of my list? Someone who was verbally abusive to my administrative assistant. (Treat everyone with respect, regardless of their position.) Someone who told a client that I was to blame for the mistake that they had made. (Take responsibility for your own mistakes.) Someone who couldn't articulate how their work makes their clients better. (It's not about you; it's about your client.)

In each of these cases, I have decided to let go. In each of those cases, I chose to confront the person before I let them go. And in each case the other person defended their actions. So three instances over thirty-plus years in the business. You will not likely have to make these decisions often, but when they do come along, it is helpful to have a solid Relationship Code in place that is built upon your organizational values.

6. *You have had a disagreement with someone.* Disagreements can be a healthy part of a working relationship and should never mean that we automatically take someone off our networking list. Disagreements are a natural part of team formation, of getting to high performance, and people with differing and strongly held beliefs will naturally disagree on things. In fact, disagreement will likely make your project better because it means that you have not been overtaken by groupthink. If you have a professional disagreement with someone and they have not violated your organizational values (see point 5), ask yourself these questions:

a. What is the velocity of the relationship? Can it withstand a disagreement?

b. Is the other person willing to openly and honestly work on the relationship in spite of the disagreement?

c. Will the disagreement improve the quality or outcome of a project?

There are only three questions to answer, but both of them are difficult. A high-velocity business relationship will likely be able to withstand some disagreement because the intensity of the forward movement will serve as momentum to keep things going. You are presumably both working toward a common goal, and the desire to get there will be incentive to overcome the disagreement. However, it is important for both parties to be able to openly and honestly work through the disagreement. It is important that both treat each other with respect and own their own responsibility within the disagreement.

Sometimes, though, disagreements make our work better when the primary motivation is to produce the best outcome.

My recommendation is to always try and work through the conflict. Even if you can't, you never know if the other person will change their mind at some point down the road. In either case, keep them on your list. Depending on the situation, you may want to slow down the velocity of the relationship, but don't let them go yet.

7. *Someone has retired.* This is frustrating. You have spent years cultivating a relationship and then they announce they are retiring and moving to a warmer climate. If you are fortunate, they introduce you to the person who is replacing them, and you cultivate a new relationship with that person. But what about the person who is retiring? Ask yourself these questions:

   a.   Do they have a large network of contacts themselves?
   b.   Have they connected you to others in their network in the past?
   c.   Are they planning to stay connected to the professional world in some way, such as board service or consulting projects?
   d.   Are they willing to share their personal contact information, including email and/or phone number?

When one of your contacts announces their retirement, be sure to ask them to include you when they send out their updated contact information. And ask what their plans are after they retire. Will they continue to serve on local boards? Will they keep their hand in the business world? Depending on their answer, there may still be opportunities to work together. For example, they may appreciate you introducing them to potential consulting clients. Even better, if you have contacts in the city to which they are moving, they may appreciate a few introductions. The decision on how to handle a connection who retires largely depends on what they want. The best approach is to ask them what they would prefer and then follow their lead. Even if they are completely in retirement mode, I keep them on my list. There is always the possibility that in the future I can help them, or they can help me.

8. *Someone has died.* You may be thinking, "They have died. Of course, I am going to take them off my list." Not so fast. Before you do, ask yourself these questions:

   a. Did this person ever connect you to anyone else?

   b. How much relationship history would be lost if you deleted this person's contact record from your list?

Every person represents a node in your overall relationship network. If one of those nodes ceases to exist, you run the risk of losing valuable relationship history. Because of this, at Outsight we have made the decision to keep deceased individuals in our database primarily because many times they are a link (or node) to many other contacts in our relationship network, and if we deleted them, that valuable information would be lost. If you have the storage capacity in your CRM system, consider keeping people on your list even after they have passed on. Set up a field that identifies the individual as deceased, and take them off your mailing list—obviously.

As a final step in developing your Relationship Code game plan, download the Let Go worksheet from www.kayedwardsauthor.com/templates and complete the following exercise. For each category of "Should We Let Go?" listed on the worksheet, identify one person from your network that falls into the category. Try to pick the person who is most representative of the types of situations you have encountered in your professional life. Then for each person, ask yourself the questions listed next to the category. Finally, write down your action strategy in the last column. Will you keep them on your list? How will you contact them next? How long before you contact them again?

You can then use the answers to these questions to define how you will respond in each situation and what your next step will be with each person you encounter in these situations. It becomes a critical part of your Relationship Code.

Congratulations, you have just created your Relationship Code.

CHAPTER 14

DEVELOPING YOUR TEAM RELATIONSHIP CODE

Y ou should now have a pretty good sense of what your individual Relationship Code is, and you are probably ready to get out and put it to use. Nice work on strengthening your network! But unless you have all the business relationships that you need, all on your own, you will need a Team Relationship Code.

Why do you need a Team Relationship Code? In the first section of this book we learned about Dunbar's Number, the theory that an individual can only maintain about 150 meaningful relationships at one time, and that 150 relationships are probably not enough to sustain the growth of your business once you account for all the different types of relationships you will need. We also learned about relationship risk, and what could happen if one person holds all of the relationship capital in an organization. We learned the importance of shared responsibility in relationship building, particularly for nonprofit organizations, or organizations where employee turnover is high, or when leaders are making succession plans.

A Team Relationship Code mitigates relationship risk for an organization. It also leverages the relationship styles of the senior team and the board. It means that everyone is doing what they do best and working together to maximize the relationship capital of the organization. It means that when one person leaves or retires, they don't take all of the relationship capital with them.

The Team Relationship Code builds on the principles of an individual Relationship Code. A Team Relationship Code requires everyone to understand their own relationship style, what is important to them, what works for them, and what they are best suited to accomplish within their own style and their own scope of responsibilities. Not everyone has the time or opportunity to be a super-networker, but everyone can contribute their strengths to the overall relationship strategy for the business.

I have come to believe that networking is not an either-or proposition; it is more nuanced. I think there are four kinds of business networking, and each of us tends to favor one type. What are they?

1. **Expanding**: This is what most of us think of as networking. It may mean going to those events and collecting a lot of business cards. It can also mean asking for referrals or intentionally putting ourselves in situations where we are likely to meet new people. The goal is to increase the total number of connections we are making to the kinds of people we want to meet.

2. **Diversifying**: This is less about total new people and more about different people: reaching into new verticals, new geographies, new cultures, or networks to which we typically don't connect. Increasing our reach exposes us to new ideas and sparks innovation. The goal is to break out of

our well-worn network silos and explore new territory. This allows serendipity to bring us new connections we might never have thought of on our own.

3. **Stabilizing**: This is about keeping relationships strong over the long term. In the consulting world, it means going back to people and organizations we have worked with and staying in touch, even if they are not currently in the market for our services. It is showing respect to the people who were once a larger part of our life. For me, this is about showing people that I value them beyond the immediate transaction of a consulting engagement.

4. **Tending**: This is deep care for the inner circle of relationships in our business lives, the people who have been there for you in your best and your worst moments, the business relationships that have become valued friendships. I want to make sure that I am continually looking for ways to show this small number of individuals how much I value them. I know someone is in my inner circle when we are no longer keeping track of who did what for whom. We are simply in it for each other.

If Dunbar's Number is a real thing, that means we need everyone to be thinking about building relationships. The CEO or sales executive shouldn't take sole responsibility for all the relationships that a business needs to grow and thrive. Why? Because each one of us brings a unique perspective on relationship building, a unique style, and connections to different groups and different kinds of people. Every one of us brings something to the relationship-building table that no one else can replace, and encouraging employees to grow and develop their own relationship-building strengths will benefit them and the business.

CONNECT PEOPLE TO COMMUNITY

Many of the relationship giants I spoke with say that community building is a natural outgrowth of their individual networking approach. Most individuals I spoke with actively think about introducing people to someone else as part of their relationship-building practice. When they meet with someone, they are assessing two things: 1) if someone in their network could provide value to the person they are meeting with, and 2) how this new person fits into the web of their network and where they would bring the most value to the network. For many, this is one of the ways they add value to those they are networking with and puts the other person at the center of the relationship. They truly believe in the power and value of a strong network of relationships, and expanding the networks of others is one of their primary goals in all their activity.

One individual said he intentionally looks for this characteristic in the people he networks with. Are they community-minded? Do they intentionally connect him to others? Most individuals I spoke with name this as one of the values they look for in others, and one of the ways they discern the character of people they meet. Most are willing to meet the first time with almost anyone, but they reserve their second meetings for people they perceive to be interested in mutual value-building, not just taking something from the relationship.

Out of this belief in the value of relationship also flows a natural ability to build community, according to several interviewees. For some, this community is a broad, informal network that looks more like a spider web than a bicycle wheel, with multiple relationships within the network forming their own connection and adding strength to the network. For others, their networking activity has created a tight-knit community of people who rely upon each other for wisdom, business referrals, problem-solving, and friendship.

One of the greatest challenges for leaders is the combination of entropy of their relationship network and over-confidence in their ability to know what they need to know to make good decisions. Research published by Dr. Paul Nutt in 1999 reported that 50 percent of executive decisions made over two decades turned out to be wrong.[1] Think about that. Half of the time your decisions have been wrong.

That same study indicates that one of the greatest predictors of erroneous decisions are *limited options*. In other words, leaders often limit their own possibilities and choose from too few options when deciding. And when they do this, their odds of being wrong increase significantly.

What does this have to do with a Team Relationship Code? Leaders who intentionally make relationship building part of their overall leadership practice tend to have broader networks, which also means they naturally come across greater subject matter expertise and more innovative ideas. It means greater access to people who are smarter than you or have experienced challenges similar to the ones you are facing and from whom you can learn, if you are willing.

The leaders I have observed who make the best decisions understand this and encourage others, not just the CEO or the chief salesperson, to build external relationships. Even if it's just one or two additional people who are intentionally engaged in external relationship building, the benefit to them and to the organization is significant.

To illustrate this, I often lead clients through an exercise of identifying their organization's Constituent Tree. A Constituent Tree is a tool for identifying all the different types of people who play a role in the success of the organization and who benefit from its success. A Constituent Tree exercise encourages you to think beyond your primary customers and consider how your organization impacts many more people than just employees and customers. The process itself is simple, but it may take some creative thinking to identify *all* the types of people who intersect with your organization.

The first type of relationship, on the left of the tree, are your Constituents. Some organizations describe them as customers, others as clients, and if you are a nonprofit organization, Constituents include both donors and those who are the recipients of your services. Most organizations have more than one type of customer, client, donor, or program recipient. The point of this exercise is to name as many of these types as you can, even if they don't often get a lot of attention from your marketing, sales, or development team.

The second type of relationship is your Participants. Participants rely directly on your organization for success as well as contribute directly to your success. Most people understand that employees rely on their organization for success. But there are many others who also rely on your organization: the family members of your employees, key vendors, or charitable organizations you support, for example. Keep thinking about this, and list as many possible relationships as you can.

The third type of relationship is those who are Vested in your organization. This group has an interest in your success because they indirectly benefit from it. A good example of this might be the local kids' sports team that your employees coach, the charitable organizations that your employees support, neighbors surrounding your office or factory. There are no right or wrong answers for these categories. The point of the exercise is to think as broadly as possible about the types of people that intersect with your organization and directly or indirectly benefit from it.

The tree shape is an apt structure for this exercise because, as you will discover, there are very few distinct lines between relationship types and a great deal of overlap. For example, one could argue that employees fit into all three categories: Constituents, Participants, and Vested. That's okay. This is a tool for thinking about relationships, and this overlap is how relationships work in practice.

The following graphic is an example of a constituent tree. Take a few minutes to think about who is on your organization's constituent tree and fill out as many different types of Constituents, Participants, and Vested relationships as you can.

- Who do you serve? (Constituents)
- Who participates directly in your success? (Participants)
- Who cares about your success? (Vested)

VESTED

STAKEHOLDERS

CONSTITUENTS

What does your Constituent Tree look like? Are there any surprises? Are there areas in which you would like to build stronger relationships? Are their more or fewer types of relationships than you thought there would be? This exercise often surprises people because it points out how many different types of people their organization touches. Even if you are a solopreneur, your work has tremendous impact and reach, and there are many different people who benefit from your success. It is also a good reminder that the task of relationship building for the success of a business is larger than one individual can usually accomplish. It takes a team.

Who is on your team? For leaders of an organization with a team of direct reports, that answer is probably easy. It is the people who report to you. For executive directors of nonprofit organizations or CEOs, the answer also includes your board of directors or board of advisors. For solopreneurs, the answer might not be as obvious. However, even for those who work alone, it is possible to engage a team around you who will network and build relationships on your behalf. In fact, every leader should think about including important referral sources from outside of their organization on their relationship-building team.

Look back at the source of your most important client or customer acquisitions over the last twelve to twenty-four months. How many of them came from personal introductions or referrals? Are there one or two (or maybe more) individuals who are a consistent source of new business? They could be part of your team. Are there vendors or other strategic partners who also serve your target customers? They could be part of your team. It is my experience that other solopreneurs or those serving in sales or account management roles are eager to find ways to partner with others outside of their organization in building relationships. Think beyond employees when engaging your team.

ENGAGING YOUR TEAM

The first step in a team Relationship Code is to identify and engage your team members. Start by making a list of who is on your team. The list should include your direct reports if you have them. If you report to a board, your list should also include your board members. And if you have important referral sources, or if you know individuals who could be referral sources, include them on the list. If you are part of a senior management team, you could include other members of your team. There is no perfect number of individuals on a relationship-building team. It could be as small as you and one other person. Keep in mind that larger teams make it harder to stay engaged and manage the process.

Think about each person on the list and their role. Is relationship building already part of their primary responsibility? For example, is their primary responsibility sales or fundraising? Is relationship building one of many responsibilities? For example, board members have a responsibility to build relationships on behalf of the organization, and it is one part of their overall role with an organization. Is relationship building new for this individual, and something they have not been asked to do previously? These individuals often have access to niche constituencies that others in your organization do not, but they will need some encouragement to think of themselves as relationship builders.

Look at each person on your list and categorize them as either 1) a primary relationship builder, someone whose job is to build relationships on behalf of the organization, 2) a secondary relationship builder, someone who has other primary responsibilities but could spend some time building relationships, or 3) a niche relationship builder, someone who does not have any relationship-building responsibility in their current role but who could connect to a niche constituency. Also, note whether this is a direct report and you have the authority to include relationship building as part of their formal job expectations, or if this is someone for whom you are engaging their assistance as a peer or colleague. This will help you understand how much time and effort each person can devote to relationship building and what kinds of support they will need from you to be effective.

Then, for each person on your list, identify what types of constituents they are best positioned to reach out to. This particularly important for your niche relationship builders. They can help you reach constituents that you may not be intentionally engaged with yet. This can also help to uncover any gaps you have in your relationship building strategy. Are all your constituencies covered with your current team? Do you need to engage an additional team member to connect to an important constituency?

Finally, think about each person's relationship-building style. What is a relationship-building style? Some of us are better at finding new relationships, expanding our networks, and always meeting new people. Others are better at maintaining and strengthening a smaller group of relationships. Do you have at least one person on your team with each of these styles? Use your best guess and list the relationship style next to each person.

This list of your team members and their relationship-building style is a draft document that you can test with your team members and use to get their input on how your organization will develop its own unique team Relationship Code.

After you have made your list, engage your team. Start by meeting with each person individually, and share your vision for relationship building and what it can accomplish for your organization. Explain that there is a limit to individual relationship building, and that it takes a collaborative effort to engage the relationships that organizations need to grow and succeed. Share what you have learned about effective relationship building, and invite them to be a part of the process for the organization. Share your Constituent Tree and your understanding of each person's relationship-building strengths.

In this meeting, you want to make sure each person understands three things:

1. Why their participation is important, and how it will not only contribute to the overall success of the organization, but to their own success as well.

2. What their specific role will be and how it fits into their overall role with the organization. If they are external to your organization, how they will benefit from partnering with your relationship building efforts.

3. What your expectations of them are. For example, how much time are you expecting them to devote to this, and how do you want them to share information about their activities? Keep it simple and doable. Even small efforts add up.

The most important thing to convey in this meeting is that everyone can be a part of relationship building, and you want them to be a part of the team, using their unique relationship building style to contribute to the overall group effort. You want to honor and celebrate all kinds of relationship-building styles and efforts because each person on your team brings something unique and important to the table. There are no good or bad relationship building styles. Every person on the team matters, and encouraging everyone's strengths is more effective than trying to turn everyone into the same kind of networker.

After each individual meeting, update your list with any feedback you have received from team members.

CONVENE YOUR TEAM

After you have met individually with each of your relationship team members, it is helpful to meet with your team as a group. If possible, include everyone on the team, even "external" referral sources. This is a great opportunity for them to get to know you and your internal team better and participate in setting relationship-building goals. This level of transparency will help to build ownership for the process you are asking them to participate in and communicates that they are a valuable part of the team.

The agenda for the meeting should include three objectives; 1) setting shared relationship goals, 2) defining the level of activity it will take to reach your goals, 3) how you will measure success.

The first agenda item is to set team goals for relationship building. There are many reasons for building business relationships, as we have seen throughout this book. Relationships help build trust, which increases the speed of business and resources. They mitigate risk, particularly if one or two individuals hold all of the customer or client relationships in the business. They hedge against the natural attrition that happens in any group of business relationships, and they introduce new ideas and creative thinking, which leads to greater innovation. Relationship goals are not just about revenue. Of course, the primary objective of every business is to maximize value. Relationships help you do that.

In addition, there are many more complimentary goals for relationship building. Some of these could include strengthening existing relationships among your existing customers. For organizations that are experiencing a high level of customer or donor attrition, strengthening relationships will help to reduce that churn. It is typically far cheaper to retain existing customers than it is to find new ones.

You may need to build relationships to gain access to information that would otherwise be difficult to attain. For example, relationships with thought leaders in your industry and other industries allow you to pick up the phone and talk to people who have a different set of knowledge than you do. Ideally, you have important knowledge to share with them too.

Relationship building can broaden the reach of your organization to new audiences, new markets, or new thought leaders. If your organization is focused in a narrow industry niche, you could adopt the relationship goal of developing connections to thought leaders in a different niche, for example, one that would allow you to branch out to other potential audiences.

Members of your team benefit from relationship building as well. It broadens their thinking, exposes them to new ideas that can spark innovation, and enhances their ability to grow. There may come a day when, in order to grow, they need to leave your firm and explore other opportunities. An expanded personal network will help them do that well.

Share the Constituent Tree exercise with the group and ask them to add any other constituent groups they can think of. Then, considering all types of constituents, ask the group to identify its goals for relationship building. A shorter list of goals that are achievable and measurable is better than an ambitious list of goals that you will not be able to achieve. One or two goals in a year is a good starting point.

What are some examples of relationship-building goals? My team has identified a goal of connecting to our clients once a week, even if it's just a quick email to update them on the progress of our project. We also set a goal of connecting to past clients at least once a year to check in on what they are doing and learn from their progress. This encourages each of us to take on some of the connecting tasks on behalf of the firm.

After you have agreed upon your goals, think about the level of activity each person will need to take on to achieve those goals. Brainstorm ideas together, and remember that defining a shorter list of activities that people will consistently accomplish is better than creating a long list of activities that will become overwhelming and discouraging in the long run. In fact, it may be helpful to generate a list of what you think you can do, and then *cut that list by two-thirds*. You can always add more activities if you find you have greater capacity. Use the steps in Section Two of this book to lead the group through the brainstorming process.

If you have any data from the previous year on relationship-building activities that you can share with the group, it will make the task easier. For example, how much time did you spend on networking in the previous year? How many people did you connect to? How many new people did you connect to? What were the results of that? What combination of activities led to your best relationships? What can you infer or extrapolate from these data that will help inform the group's thinking? And if you don't have any data, that's okay too. Asking the group to think about these questions can also be very informative and help you think about what activities and how much activity will help achieve your goals.

How much activity is enough? That will differ for each person and for every team. If you have relationship-building data from previous years, and someone on your team who is skilled at data analysis, you can build a regression model that can help identify the correlations between activities and revenue, for example. And if that sounds way too complicated and you don't have any data to evaluate, that's okay too. Now is the perfect time to start thinking about what kinds of data you will collect and how you will organize it so that you can learn from it moving forward. I have found that "how much is enough" is hard to quantify, and this is another place where we at Outsight often experiment with activity goals for six months or so, then we look back and brainstorm about what activities produced results and what didn't.

The right level of activity is what each individual on the team is comfortable taking on and following through on, and what the group thinks will collectively move them on the path to their relationship goals. Any starting point is better than no activity. Later on, you can reevaluate your goals and your progress and make adjustments. It's better to try something for a few months and see how it goes than to get too focused on the numbers and end up not doing anything at all.

The next step is to agree on how you will capture information about individuals and your interactions with them. Most organizations already use some kind of CRM system to manage their relationships. If you are a solopreneur, you may be using Outlook or something similar to manage your contacts. Even a simple, low-cost CRM system will typically provide the ability to customize fields and track the kinds of information you need to build relationships as a team. Whatever system you use should be accessible to everyone on the team. If your team includes individuals outside of your organization, you can decide to give them access using role-based security to limit that access to information that is appropriate for them. Or you can decide to ask them to share information on relationship-building activities via email or some other simple method. Google forms are often an easy-to-implement solution for data collection via the web.

Keep your system as simple as possible. It will only be an effective system if it gets used, so design it for the person on the team who is least likely to use it. In addition to basic contact information for each record—including email, phone, and city—the minimum viable information needs to include the following:

- **Referral source:** How were you introduced to this person?
- **Connection:** How does this person know you? How close is the relationship? (see chapter 5)
- **Alignment:** How closely does this person align with your target persona and your organizational values? (see chapter 5)
- **Velocity:** Is the relationship speeding up or slowing down? (see chapter 5)
- **Next Steps:** When and how will you reach out to this person next?

The goal of the discussion with your team is to agree on a system for capturing this information that is not so complicated or difficult that no one will use it. Start with the minimum amount of effort needed, and if that works well, you can always add more information later.

Finally, agree on what success looks like. In defining success, it is helpful to think about what you can control in relationship building and what you can't. You can control how many times you reach out to people, the way in which you reach out, the kinds of people you reach out to, and how you respond when people reach out to you. You can't control how people respond to you, how often they respond, or whether or not they do what you ask them to do. That means your definition of success needs to focus on the things that you can control: your own actions.

As your team defines success, success means that you have executed the relationship-building activities that you set out to do. Success looks like an if/then statement: "If we engage fifty new relationships this year, then we will increase the total number of requests for quotes that we receive." In research terms, success is a hypothesis that you are testing. It is important to clearly define what success looks like because it will give you the opportunity to examine if your assumptions about relationship building are true. It is possible that you do all of the relationship-building activities you set out to do and still don't meet your goals. That becomes a learning opportunity for you and your team, a chance to examine your activities and make changes in your activities. But if you don't define success in clear terms of "if we do this activity, then this will happen," you will have no opportunity to learn from your experience and adjust.

Please note that this assumes that everything else is working well (for example, your product meets a real need in the marketplace, it is perceived as a good value for the money, and you are creating great customer experiences). All the relationship building in the world will not help if any of these are going wrong.

Conclude your meeting by agreeing how often you are going to meet as a team. Ongoing team meetings are an opportunity to compare notes, report on progress, and make adjustments to your Team Relationship Code. Use these meetings to celebrate what is going well, and learn from what hasn't gone the way you expected. Affirm each member of your team for their relationship strengths and encourage their progress. Meet only as often as you need to encourage and celebrate successes, and provide time to troubleshoot challenges and roadblocks for individual team members. The goal is to build relationships, not spend all of your time talking about building relationships.

Congratulations! You now have a Team Relationship Code in place.

KEY TAKEAWAYS

- The value of a Team Relationship Code is its ability to exponentially grow the number of high-quality relationships a senior team can manage.
- Most organizations have more types of relationships to manage than any one person can handle.
- Every person brings different relationship-building strengths and has access to different networks. Everyone can participate in some way.
- Define what success looks like, and measure activities that will lead to success. Check your assumptions along the way.
- Set manageable goals, and don't take on more than you can accomplish.
- Use team time efficiently to celebrate successes and troubleshoot challenges. Spend more time on relationship building than talking about relationship building.
- Make it fun.

CHAPTER 15

HONORING RELATIONSHIPS AS YOU LEAVE YOUR LEGACY

J ust like your network may be retiring and moving to Florida, there will come a day when you retire and move to Florida (or whatever your idea of the perfect retirement place is). For some of us, the thought of retirement is either something that seems very far away, or something we prefer not to think about. It can represent a loss of position, personal value, and especially the professional relationships that are rewarding.

Who should be thinking about leaving a relationship legacy? The short answer to this is everyone. Everyone who relies on trusted relationships to grow and sustain their business should think about how to end those relationships well and pass them on to someone else who will care for them.

There are several specific circumstances that will benefit significantly from thinking intentionally about relationship legacy because they tend to be more dependent on the relationship-building capacity of a single leader.

1. *Professional service firms are often led by a charismatic founder who has built the business through his or her network of relationships.* They are the brand of the firm and the one who everyone thinks of when they think of the firm. They are often the biggest rainmaker, and the systems and structures of the firm have been built around supporting their success and their style of relationship building. Too many of these firms falter or die when this founder retires because no one else does it quite like them. Anyone else is trying to fill a set of shoes that will never fit.

2. *Founder-led organizations are like professional service firms in that their systems and structures are often built around a singular style of relationship cultivation.* Even larger firms or nonprofits that are founder-led can fall into the trap of relying on the founder's values and style to dictate relationship building culture. Because no two individuals are alike, the next leader will have a different style. Sometimes boards deliberately choose a successor who is the opposite of the founder, overcompensating for any perceived faults in an effort to fix what might be going wrong at the end of the founder's tenure. This leads to a disconnect between the new leader and the key relationships of the organization.

3. *Family-owned businesses often wish to pass the business to the next generation without recognizing the importance of the relationship network held by the current generation of leadership.* The trust embedded in these relationships doesn't automatically transfer to the next generation just because they have inherited the formal title of CEO.

4. *When key board members step away from an active board role, their relationships often go with them.* This is especially true for nonprofit organizations. By intentionally making all board members part of the networking team, whether they are actively raising money or not, and tracking their relationship building activity as outlined in this book, their connections are more likely to stay with the organization. In addition, the organization is more likely to select a new board member who aligns with the networking style of the previous board member, which helps to preserve the relationship capacity of the organization through the transition.

These are just a few of the situations in which it is important to consider how a leader's relationship capital and capability will be preserved for the organization.

Yet so few organizations think intentionally about this. Few leaders take the time to make a relationship transfer plan when they make their succession plans. I know I have struggled with how to do this. It's so much easier to ignore the inevitable, focus on more immediate challenges, and pretend that the end of my leadership and my life isn't coming. In this chapter I will share some things that I have learned along the way from others who have done it well, and the steps that I am applying as I face this time in my career.

HONOR YOUR RELATIONSHIPS

According to Meriam Webster, the definition of *honor* is "to regard or treat (someone) with admiration and respect."[1] Honor is the great gift we can give to those who have helped us in our business success. It is an important part of expressing gratitude to people for what they have done for us. At the end of our careers, we want to know that we have made a difference in people's lives, that we have left a legacy. Intentionally honoring others, reminding them of how important they have been to us, is a way for us to do that. When we honor others, that honor reflects on us. It is like a seed we sow in others whose yield becomes the evidence of our legacy.

What does that look like? I once attended a charity dinner as a guest of one of the board members, someone I have known as a business associate for many years, including serving on a board with him. As we went around the table, each sharing how we were connected to our host, he shared that I had introduced him to the person who helped him start his current firm. He also said that had been a turning point for him and his success. Even though I had completely forgotten about making that introduction, that one simple story told many years later left me feeling honored and seen and deeply grateful for having known this colleague.

The way in which you hand off your relationships can pay respect and admiration to others for what they have contributed to your business and to your career. You can choose to do this intentionally, or you can choose not to. What you sow into your relationships at the end of your career will be part of your legacy. We can't expect others to honor us if we don't first honor them.

Every relationship is different, and honor will mean different things for different people. Everyone deserves your respect, but not every relationship warrants the same amount of time and effort in the hand-off process. Match what the relationships means to you with the way you hand it off. For example, the former client with whom I exchange an email or two every year is different than the trusted colleague who I work with on multiple projects every year. The former client is important, and I will likely introduce him or her to one of my team members via email and suggest they have a cup of coffee to get to know each other. In contrast, I will take significant time honoring the trusted colleague and making sure I communicate how much the relationship has meant to me and how they have contributed to my personal journey. I will also give them ample notice of my plans for stepping back, communicate how my team will continue to work with them, and give them many opportunities to input what they would like the relationship to look like in the future, and what they need moving forward.

Celebration plays a major role in honoring relationships well. Too often we rush to the handing-off part and forget to celebrate in a meaningful way what was good about the relationship, and how the other person has brought benefit to our lives. In healthy, close relationships where we are always communicating and always appreciating the other, there is a risk that we miss the importance of that final celebration, the opportunity to leave the other with a fuller sense of the meaning of the relationship in its entirety.

We also need to give the other person the opportunity to celebrate us, to share with us how we have impacted their lives for good. Especially as we transition from a working role to a different phase in life, it is helpful to have others reinforce that we have created good in the world, and that we are worthy people. I think it is hard-wired into our natures to want to know that our lives have purpose and can continue to have purpose even as we move onto new roles.

A beautiful story of celebrating relationships well is told by Eugene O'Kelly, the late chairman of KPMG. After being diagnosed with an incurable brain tumor and being told he had only a few months to live, O'Kelly intentionally wound down his relationships, saying goodbye to everyone who was important to him in a way that was uniquely meaningful to each relationship, starting with work colleagues and ending with his wife and only child. He documented this approach in his posthumous book, *Chasing Daylight*: "In each case, I expressed my appreciation and gratitude. And I tried to focus on something especially meaningful about our relationship."[2]

While most of us will not have to deal with such a dramatic end to our professional relationships, O'Kelly's story is a remarkable reminder that we can leave our work relationships with honor, for the other as well as for ourselves.

When my husband passed away after a long illness, when we finally moved him to hospice care, we didn't know that he would go from joking around with the kids to unresponsive within a few hours. We didn't know there was no time to say goodbye. My husband told me every day of our marriage, without fail, that he loved me. I don't doubt it for a second. I deeply regret that we couldn't, one last time, tell each other what the sum total of our thirty-three years together meant to us.

FOUR STEPS TO PLANNING YOUR RELATIONSHIP LEGACY

Just like you will create an intentional succession plan for handing off every other aspect of your leadership role, your relationships should have a "succession plan." This plan should consider the character of the relationship and what it brings to your business. It will provide a roadmap for how, when, and to whom you hand off your relationships. And like all good roadmaps, it will tell you where you are on your journey.

A relationship succession process includes four steps: 1) prioritize, 2) start early, 3) make connections, and 4) let go. Each one of these steps can be mapped out in greater detail.

PRIORITIZE

Just like you prioritized your relationship types when creating your Relationship Code, prioritization is an important part of leaving a relationship legacy. Some relationships are more important to the future success of the business than others. It doesn't mean that all the people you know aren't equally valuable as human beings. It just means that some will play a larger role in the future success of the business. By prioritizing those relationships, you are being a good steward of your time and relationship capital and leaving a much more valuable relationship legacy.

Start by reviewing all your Key Relationship types and asking yourself which ones have contributed the most to your personal and business success, and how that might change in the future version of the business. You may be handing off your relationships to more than one person. In that case, the priorities might be different for different people. Make a list of your Key Relationship types and order them from highest to lowest priority based on the *future* state of the business. This is the first step in prioritization.

As you began your Relationship Code journey, these categories provided some helpful guidelines for how much time and effort to devote to cultivating each type of audience. As you create a plan for leaving a relationship legacy, you will go one step further and consider the 150 or so individuals who are the most important to you and the future success of your business. Then, intentionally hand off these relationships in a way that honors what they have meant to you and your business.

Think about these relationships as a triangle. At the top of the triangle are the ten to fifteen people who have contributed the most to your professional and business success. In the middle are fifteen to forty people who represent the next tier of importance. You may know them well and have frequent interactions with them, but they aren't quite in the same category of importance as the top tier. On the bottom are the remaining one hundred or so people who have played a significant role in your business.

These triangles may look something like this.

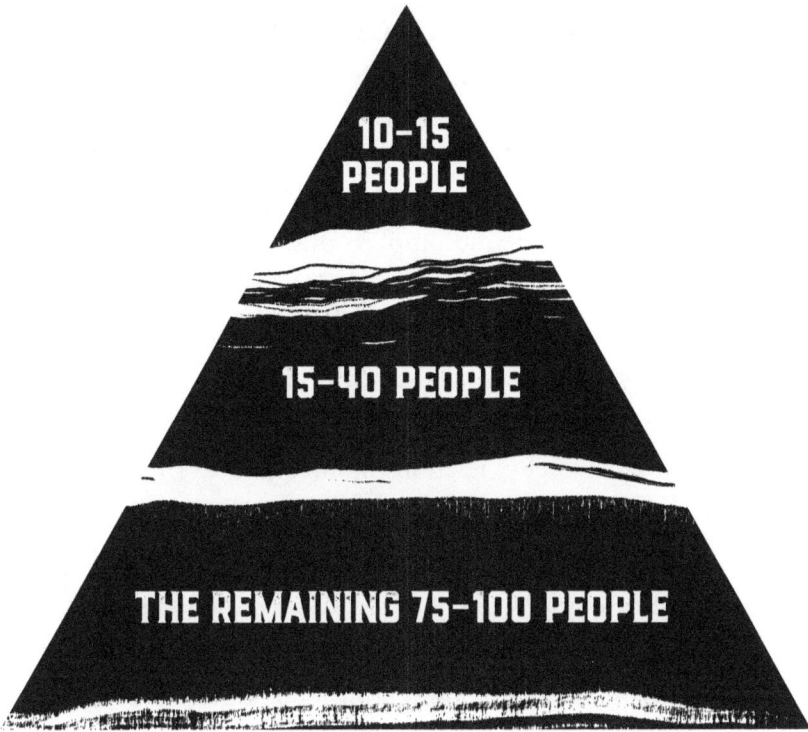

Take some time to review the people you interact with most frequently as part of your professional role and make some judgements about where each person belongs in the pyramid. This will be your guide for how you hand off your relationships.

CONCENTRIC CIRCLES OF
RELATIONSHIPS

Part of being a relationship giant is the challenge of managing an ever-growing network. When I asked these individuals how they accomplish this, many bought up the concept of concentric circles. Not every relationship is the same, and many of these relationship giants talk about varying levels of investment in their relationships. Not everyone is in the inner circle, and not everyone gets the same level of relationship investment. They each recognize this as part of the limitation of being human.

One described his relationships as either episodic, seasonal, or long term. Some relational interaction happened once. They were valuable, but they won't happen again. Some relational interactions go on for a season, in which two individuals are working together on a specific task. And other interactions become long-term relationships.

For many, the closest circle of relationships consists of those that started as business relationships and then became personal friendships. These are characterized by the relationships in which they interact with each other's spouses and families. One interviewee, for example, said that if he doesn't know a spouse's name, it doesn't count as a relationship. Or they go through personal struggles together. One individual characterized business relationships a those that have a beginning and an end, and the business relationships that continue for the long term have become friendships.

START EARLY

It takes time and energy to hand off a relationship well. It will take considerable time to get through your list of relationships, and you will want to make sure you leave enough time at the end of your tenure for the people who you are closest to. There is no "one size fits all" plan for leaving a relationship legacy, and your path will look different than anyone else's, so start early and give yourself plenty of time to do it well. You can adjust along the way and speed up the process, or slow it down in whatever way works for you. The objective is to get to the end of your career and feel like the relationship legacy you are leaving will benefit everyone in the relationship, including you.

The idea is to act with intentionality based on each type of relationship. Start at the bottom of the triangle, and plan to spend the most time and effort at the top of the triangle. In practice, this means that you hand off each individual relationship in a way that honors the person and honors the relationship and how important it is to you and your firm.

It is important to remember that there may also be many relationships that have transcended business and become personal friends. The goal of this process is not to end the friendships but to honor the role that these people have played in the success of your business and professional life. You will want to find ways for the friendships to continue even when you are no longer working together.

By starting early on this process, as soon as you are thinking about handing off your leadership roles, you allow yourself time to carefully plan how you will hand off each relationship to someone else on your senior team. You may even find that the process helps to identify relationship gaps in your senior team. Are there relationship skills and strengths that you need to build up within your team? Planning ahead gives you the time to mentor or hire the skills your team will need to be successful.

Estimate the amount of time you have before you step away from your relational role, and plan to spend about a third of that time on each tier of the pyramid. Because there are more relationships at the bottom of the pyramid, you will naturally spend less time handing off each of those relationships and spend the most time with your top ten to fifteen relationships. Starting early allows you to get a sense of how much time investment the process is taking so you can adjust your timeline accordingly. It also allows you to continue to model good relationship building and mentor your team throughout the process.

MAKE GOOD INTRODUCTIONS

Making good introductions means that others are no longer dependent on you to keep the relationship going. What good is it to try to hand off a relationship if you are still core to its healthy functioning? Everything that goes into creating a good relationship, everything I have shared so far in this book, also applies to the process of handing off relationships well.

Good relationships are built on a foundation of shared values. As you go through your list of important relationships and think about how to and to whom you are going to hand them off, look first for values alignment. No matter how well you hand off the relationship, if the values of both parties are not aligned, it will never work out in the long term. People may express them differently, be at different stages in their careers, or have wildly different personalities, but if their values align, they are much more likely to form a lasting relationship.

As the one who is making the initial introduction, it is important to know what each party brings to the relationship, and what each one needs. It is your job to make the initial assessment that the skills and strengths are complementary, and that there is a possibility that in bringing these two people together, the combination will yield a greater good than either one of them could accomplish alone. Rosabeth Moss Kanter describes this as "interdependence" based on her research of successful corporate alliances around the world. She discovered that interdependence is one of the eight factors that predict a healthy alliance. "The partners need each other. They have complementary assets and skills. Neither can accomplish alone what both can together."[3]

When you make the introduction, help get the relationship off to a good start by naming a "mutual why." Tell both parties why you think this will be a good relationship fit and how each of them is working toward a similar goal or *why*. Then explain how those goals could possibly align and create mutual benefit. Kanter also points to "importance" as one of the eight factors that make for healthy alliances. "The relationship fits major strategic objectives of the partners, so they want to make it work. Partners have long-term goals in which the relationship plays a key role."[4]

In addition, as I have pointed out earlier, great relationships happen when people have something meaningful to do together, something that they both value and both derive benefit from. When making introductions, you may see this possibility more clearly than the people you are introducing. After all, you are the one who knows both of them, and you are putting them together for a reason, so make that reason as explicit as possible, even if it is something simple. For example, you could say something like, "John, this is Susan. She is working on an affordable housing project that you may be interested in. Susan, this is John. His company is located in the area in which you are working. I think the two of you should have coffee together and learn more about each other." Suggesting a coffee date is a simple first step that two people can do, and suggesting something specific increases the likelihood that John and Susan will connect.

LET GO

When you have done everything you can to make the introduction and get the relationship off to a good start, it is time to let go. This may be the most difficult part of handing off your relationships. You care about both people you have introduced, and you want to see them benefit from this relationship. But you have to step back and let them develop their own relationship without you to make it work.

Among my clients, I have seen leaders take one of three different approaches to this point in one's career. The first approach is to do nothing and hope for the best. Rather than face the discomfort of acknowledging that one's business career, and its relationships, are going to change, we can pretend that things will go on as they are forever. Until they don't. The leader either simply retires without any intentional care for his or her relationships, or worse, an unexpected illness or death forces them to end without intention.

The second approach is when the leader finds another person, just like themselves, and expects them to pick up where the leader left off. This "mini me" approach almost never works because there are no two people who are exactly alike. Too many times I have seen a leader cycle through multiple versions of an heir apparent, none of them ever quite living up to the expectations of them, resulting in personal, professional, and relational damage that could have been avoided.

The third approach is more successful. It multiplies the relationship-building strengths of the leader by sowing them into multiple people, much like a seed multiplies when it is sown in a field. The various relational assets that the leader brought to the table can be nurtured in a team, with each team member using his or her strengths to carry on a portion of the relationship legacy being passed on to them. This not only sustains the existing relational capital, it grows it exponentially.

The goal of engaging your team in relationship building is to create an intentional way for leaders to pass on the relationship capital that they have built up for the benefit of the next generation of leaders. The goal of passing off your relationships with intentionality is to honor the people who have contributed to your success and leave a relationship legacy

We are often tempted to stick around in the relationship just to be helpful. I know you have the best of intentions in doing this. You want the relationship to be successful. You care about both parties you have introduced, and you want them both to benefit from this new relationship. Don't do it. Don't be tempted by this. Whether it's because you want to feel valued, helpful, or perhaps you don't quite trust the two of them to make this work, it is never a good idea to stay in a relationship in an open-ended way. When you are handing off business relationships, your goal is to give the ones you are handing them to the freedom to make the relationship work. Don't hang around and potentially mess that up. The relationship will succeed or fail based on the values and efforts of the two new people in it, and it is no longer yours to steward, which is often difficult to manage because we love being needed and feeling in control. Of course there will be those relationships that have gone beyond business to personal friendships, and you will continue to stay close to the friends you have welcomed into your personal life. I am not suggesting you end those relationships.

I have seen so many organizations ask the founder to stay around and serve on the board, or the outgoing board chair is asked to sit in on meetings. It sounds like a good idea at the time because it is our nature to resist change, and setting up a "half-in/half-out" role for the one leaving the relationship satisfies our need to keep things the same. The problem with this new role is that it usually looks and functions just like the old role, which means that the new leader never has the freedom he or she needs to succeed on their own. In most cases, it is best not to try to stick around. The only way I have ever seen it work well is if there is a new, clearly defined role for you in the relationship that the other two people have requested you to fulfill, and you can execute that role without slipping back into your old relationship habits.

If you have discerned well and put two people together whose values align, and you have set them up for success by suggesting a simple thing they can do together, then you need to trust them to figure it out. It will either work or it won't. You are handing off the relationship and your scope of authority over it, so it is time to let go and trust. If you think one of the people in the relationship needs a little help, give them a copy of this book.

Just like any change we experience in life, when you hand off a relationship, there will be new things that come into your life as a result. You are creating space for the next stage of your life, post-business relationships, and you have a choice about how you will respond to it. You can choose to cherish the new things that come into your life. Yes, they will be different. Yes, the transition may be difficult. But you have proven many times before that you are capable of facing new circumstances and challenges, and you can choose to do that again with joy and grace. You can choose to be open and welcoming of the new that you are making space for while trusting that you have handed off relationships in a way that brings joy and grace to others. Well done.

CONCLUSION

Some of the most meaningful aspects of our careers are the people we have worked with, the relationships we have made, and the positive impact we have made on others' lives. You believe this because you made the time to read this book. Perhaps you picked it up because you wanted to grow your business, or you picked it up because you wanted to help your team do a better job building professional relationships, or some completely different reason. The reason doesn't matter. What matters is that some part of you already understood how important the people we work with are, and you wanted to make that part of your life better.

I hope that you found this book helpful. I hope that you recognize that no matter where you are in your journey of building professional relationships, you are making progress. We are all on a journey, and we are all getting better at it every day.

My greatest hope is that you take one thing from this book, one new way of looking at relationships, or one new habit, and make it a part of your relationship building life.

KEY TAKEAWAYS

- Honoring people in how you leave your relationship legacy is just as important as any other aspect of your succession/end-of-career planning.
- Start by appreciating and celebrating the people who have helped you along your career journey and contributed to your success. Make sure they know how important they have been to you.

- Prioritizing and carefully planning how you hand off relationships will set up your business or your team for success in the future. Start early, and give it the time it deserves.
- Help the people you are handing relationships to by making good introductions and knowing how to let go and trust.

ACKNOWLEDGMENTS

A BIG THANK-YOU TO MY PACK

Many thanks to everyone who helped me get this book across the finish line. Steve Brock, for his wisdom and expertise. Thank you for reading every word of this book and giving me honest, incredibly helpful feedback. For coaching me through the process and for your friendship, thank you. You are my dear brother in Christ, and I am honored to journey with you.

Thank you to my team—Sarah Kerkman, Rebecca Mattox, Sam Mattox, and Mary Reinders—for your feedback and edits to the manuscript and being there for me through losing the most important relationship of my life. I could not have done this without you. Sarah, thank you for affirming that you will have to pry that Oxford comma out of my cold, dead hands, and for deciphering my crazy handwriting.

Thanks to my dear friends and business coaches, Mark Vincent and Kristin Evenson. Mark, there are no words to thank you for everything you have done to help me on my journey. Kristin, you are a dear sister and courageous friend.

To the fellow Convene CEOs, thank you for believing in me and inspiring this book. Krysta DeBoer, Ben Mott, Dave Smith, and Mike Tenpas, you are my heroes.

To the inspirational relationship builders I have learned from along the way—Linda Maris, Brenda Skelton, Ed McDowell, John Stanley, and so many others—thank you for being shining examples of how to do this with integrity and honor.

And thank you to the master networkers who graciously agreed to let me pick their brains and learn from their networking styles. Some of them agreed to be acknowledged, and some of them have not. Below are some of these master networkers. If you are fortunate enough to cross paths with them, pay attention to how they are building and nurturing relationships.

Bryce Baker, CFP
Lead Advisor
Brighton Jones
www.brightonjones.com

Norm Edwards
Retired Advancement Officer

Dr. Daniel Hallak
Chief Commercial Officer
WiLD Leaders
www.wildleaders.org

Bob King
Principal
C.O.O. Services, LLC
www.cooservices.com

Kirby Langley
Vice President of Sales

ENDNOTES

INTRODUCTION

1   Gal Beckerman, *The Quiet Before: On the Unexpected Origins of Radical Ideas* (New York: Crown Publishing, 2022).

2   Wisdom Portal, "Stories of the Human Spirit," *https://www.wisdomportal.com/Technology/TSEliot-TheRock.html.*

3   Frank Zappa with Peter Occhiogrosso, *The Real Frank Zappa Book* (New York: Poseidon Press, 1989), 139

4   C. S. Lewis, *The Great Divorce* (New York, NY, Macmillan Publishing Company, 1946), 21.

CHAPTER 1

1   "Relational Capital," Wikipedia, last modified January 22, 2024, https://en.wikipedia.org/wiki/Relational_capital.

2   "Metcalf's Law," Wikipedia, last modified January 29, 2024, https://en.wikipedia.org/wiki/Metcalfe%27s_law.

3   "Beckstrom's Law," Wikipedia, last modified January 13, 2024 https://en.wikipedia.org/wiki/Beckstrom%27s_law.

4   https://www.merriam-webster.com/dictionary/intentional

5   Dunbar, Robin, *Grooming, Gossip, and the Evolution of Language* (Cambridge, Massachusetts: Harvard University Press, 1998,) 77.

6   Adam Grant, *Give and Take,* (Penquin Books, New York, NY), 5

7   Shalom H. Schwartz and Anat Bardi, "Values Hierarchies Across Cultures: Taking a Similarities Perspective," *Journal of Cross Cultural Psychology* 32 (May 2001), https://doi.org/10.1177/0022022101032003002.

8   Ibid.

9   *Cultural Psychology* 32 (May 2001), HYPERLINK \l "bookmark2"https://doi.org/10.1177/00220221010320030

10 Mark S. Granovetter, "The Strength of Weak Ties," *American Journal of Sociology*, Volume 78, Issue 6 (May, 1973)

11 Dr. Henry Cloud, *Boundaries* (Grand Rapids, Michigan, Zondervan, 2017), 45.

12 Susan Scott, *Fierce Conversations* (New York, NY, Published by The Berkley Publishing Group, A division of Penguin Group Inc., 2002), 213.

CHAPTER 2

1   C.S. Lewis, *The Great Divorce* (New York, NY, Touchstone, 1946), 20.
2   Wendy McClelland, *Why I Say No to Coffee Meetings,* April 7, 2024 https://www.linkedin.com/pulse/20140407211445-1221046-why-i-say-no-to-coffee-meetings/.

CHAPTER 3

1   Bob Burg, *The Go-Giver: A Little Story About A Powerful Idea* (New York, NY, Portfolio, 2007), 25.
2   Stephen M. R. Covey, *The Speed of Trust* (New York, NY, Free Press, 2006), 17.
3   Peter Drucker, *Innovation and Entrepreneurship, Practice and Principles* (New York, NY, Harper & Row, Publishers, Inc., 1985), 35.
4   Eric von Hippel, Stefan Thomke, and Mary Sonnack, "Creating Breakthroughs at 3M," *Harvard Business Review*, September–October 1999, 47.
5   Mike Salokas, interview by author, March 17, 2020.

CHAPTER 4

1   James E. Austin and The Peter F. Drucker Foundation for Nonprofit Management, The Collaboration Challenge: How Nonprofits and Businesses Succeed Through Alliances (New York, NY, John Wiley & Sons, 2000), 61.

CHAPTER 5

1   Roy F. Baumeister, John Tierney, *Willpower* (New York, New York, Penguin Group, Inc., 2011), 168.
2   Andy Lopata, *Connected Leadership: How Professional Relationships Underpin Executive Success* (Panoma Press Limited, St. Albans, Herts, UK, 2020), 96.
3   Oguz A. Acar, Murat Tarakci, and Daan van Knippenberg, "Creativity and Innovation Under Constraints: A Cross-Disciplinary Integrative Review," *Journal of Management*, Volume 45, Issue 1, January 2019.

CHAPTER 6

1   William Landes Foster, Peter Kim, & Barbara Christiansen,"Ten Nonprofit Funding Models," *Stanford Social Innovation Review*, Spring 2009, https://ssir.org/articles/entry/ten_nonprofit_funding_models

CHAPTER 7

1   Michael Porter and Nitin Nohria, "How CEOs Spend Their Time," *Harvard Business Review*, July-August 2018

2   Dr. Ivan Misner, "How Much Time Should You Spend Networking?" https://ivanmisner.com/time-spend-networking/.

CHAPTER 8

1   Steve R. Covey, *The Speed of Trust* (New York, NY, Free Press, An Imprint of Simon & Schuster, Inc., 2018), 13.
2   Mirroring, https://en.wikipedia.org/wiki/Mirroring.
3   Ghosting, https://en.wikipedia.org/wiki/Ghosting_(behavior).
4   Grant Hilary Brenner, MD, DFAPA, "Why Are You Always Thinking About Yourself?" *Psychology Today*, January 19, 2018.

CHAPTER 9

1   Mark Travers Ph.D., "Happiness Comes from Making Others Feel Good," *Psychology Today*, May 27, 2021.
2   Jecker, J., & Landy, D. (1969). "Liking a Person as a Function of Doing Him a Favor. *Human Relations*," *22*(4), 371–378.
3   Benjamin Franklin, *Franklin's Autobiography*, Edited by O. Leon Reid (American Book Company, New York, NY, 1896), 44.

CHAPTER 10

1   Nicholas J. Webb, *What Customers Crave: How to Create Relevant and Memorable Experiences at Every Touchpoint* (AMACOM, October 13, 2016), 1.

CHAPTER 14

1   Dr. Paul C. Nutt, "Surprising but true: Half the decisions in organizations fail," Academy of Management Executive, 1999, Vol 13, No. 4.

CHAPTER 15

1   https://www.merriam-webster.com/dictionary/honor#dictionary-entry-1
2   Eugene O'Kelly, *Chasing Daylight* (McGraw-Hill, New York, NY, 2006), 110.
3   Rosabeth Moss Kanter, "Collaborative Advantage: Successful partnerships manage the relationship, not just the deal," *Harvard Business Review*, July-August 1994, p. 100.
4   Rosabeth Moss Kanter, "Collaborative Advantage: Successful partnerships manage the relationship, not just the deal," Harvard Business Review, July-August 1994, p.100.

ABOUT THE AUTHOR

KAY EDWARDS is a committed introvert who has built a successful thirty-plus-year consulting career by learning how to develop trusted professional relationships. Her firm, Outsight Network, helps leaders with what they need to know and who they need to know to achieve their missions. You can learn more about Kay at KayEdwardsAuthor. com.

www.ingramcontent.com/pod-product-compliance
Lightning Source LLC
Chambersburg PA
CBHW030516210326
41597CB00013B/924